UNDERSTANDING CHUCK PALAHNIUK

UNDERSTANDING CONTEMPORARY AMERICAN LITERATURE

Matthew J. Bruccoli, Founding Editor

Linda Wagner-Martin, Series Editor

Volumes on

Edward Albee | Sherman Alexie | Nelson Algren | Paul Auster
Nicholson Baker | John Barth | Donald Barthelme | The Beats
Thomas Berger | The Black Mountain Poets | Robert Bly | T. C. Boyle
Truman Capote | Raymond Carver | Michael Chabon | Fred Chappell
Chicano Literature | Contemporary American Drama
Contemporary American Horror Fiction
Contemporary American Literary Theory
Contemporary American Science Fiction, 1926–1970
Contemporary American Science Fiction, 1970–2000
Contemporary Chicana Literature | Pat Conroy | Robert Coover | Don DeLillo
Philip K. Dick | James Dickey | E. L. Doctorow | Rita Dove | Dave Eggers
Louise Erdrich | John Gardner | George Garrett | Tim Gautreaux | William Gibson
John Hawkes | Joseph Heller | Lillian Hellman | Beth Henley | James Leo Herlihy
David Henry Hwang | John Irving | Randall Jarrell | Gish Jen | Charles Johnson
Diane Johnson | Edward P. Jones | Adrienne Kennedy | William Kennedy | Jack Kerouac
Jamaica Kincaid | Etheridge Knight | Tony Kushner | Ursula K. Le Guin
Jonathan Lethem | Denise Levertov | Bernard Malamud | David Mamet
Bobbie Ann Mason | Colum McCann | Cormac McCarthy | Jill McCorkle
Carson McCullers | W. S. Merwin | Arthur Miller | Stephen Millhauser | Lorrie Moore
Toni Morrison's Fiction | Vladimir Nabokov | Gloria Naylor | Joyce Carol Oates
Tim O'Brien | Flannery O'Connor | Cynthia Ozick | Suzan-Lori Parks | Walker Percy
Katherine Anne Porter | Richard Powers | Reynolds Price | Annie Proulx
Thomas Pynchon | Ron Rash | Adrienne Rich | Theodore Roethke | Philip Roth
Richard Russo | May Sarton | Hubert Selby, Jr. | Mary Lee Settle | Sam Shepard
Neil Simon | Isaac Bashevis Singer | Jane Smiley | Gary Snyder | William Stafford
Robert Stone | Anne Tyler | Gerald Vizenor | Kurt Vonnegut
David Foster Wallace | Robert Penn Warren | James Welch | Eudora Welty
Edmund White | Colson Whitehead | Tennessee Williams
August Wilson | Charles Wright

UNDERSTANDING

CHUCK PALAHNIUK

Douglas Keesey

The University of South Carolina Press

Published by the University of South Carolina Press
Columbia, South Carolina 29208

uscpress.com

Printed in the United States of America

Library of Congress Cataloging-in-Publication Data
can be found at http://catalog.loc.gov/.

ISBN 978-1-61117-697-1 (cloth)
ISBN 978-1-61117-698-8 (ebook)

For my wife and partner
All of this is really about Helen Bailey

CONTENTS

Series Editor's Preface ix

Acknowledgments xi

Chapter 1
Understanding Chuck Palahniuk 1

Chapter 2
The Struggle for Identity: *Fight Club, Invisible Monsters, Survivor, Choke* 15

Chapter 3
The Horror Trilogy: *Lullaby, Diary, Haunted* 50

Chapter 4
Teen Terrors: *Rant, Pygmy* 68

Chapter 5
Porn Bodies and Romantic Myths: *Snuff, Tell-All, Beautiful You* 81

Chapter 6
Palahniuk's Divine Comedy: *Damned, Doomed* 101

Notes 117

Bibliography 125

Index 135

SERIES EDITOR'S PREFACE

The Understanding Contemporary American Literature series was founded by the estimable Matthew J. Bruccoli (1931–2008), who envisioned these volumes as guides or companions for students as well as good nonacademic readers, a legacy that will continue as new volumes are developed to fill in gaps among the nearly one hundred series volumes published to date and to embrace a host of new writers only now making their marks on our literature.

As Professor Bruccoli explained in his preface to the volumes he edited, because much influential contemporary literature makes special demands, "the word understanding in the titles was chosen deliberately. Many willing readers lack an adequate understanding of how contemporary literature works; that is, of what the author is attempting to express and the means by which it is conveyed." Aimed at fostering this understanding of good literature and good writers, the criticism and analysis in the series provide instruction in how to read certain contemporary writers—explicating their material, language, structures, themes, and perspectives—and facilitate a more profitable experience of the works under discussion.

In the twenty-first century Professor Bruccoli's prescience gives us an avenue to publish expert critiques of significant contemporary American writing. The series continues to map the literary landscape and to provide both instruction and enjoyment. Future volumes will seek to introduce new voices alongside canonized favorites, to chronicle the changing literature of our times, and to remain, as Professor Bruccoli conceived, contemporary in the best sense of the word.

Linda Wagner-Martin, Series Editor

ACKNOWLEDGMENTS

This book would never have been completed without the vital support of certain key individuals, and it is a pleasure to have the opportunity to acknowledge their contributions. First, I wish to express my gratitude to Linda Wagner-Martin. Her initial enthusiasm for this book inspired me, and her continued belief in it was sustaining. I am also grateful to Jim Denton and Linda Fogle at the University of South Carolina Press for their faith in this work and for their expert advice along the way.

At Cal Poly, English Department Chair Kathryn Rummell and Dean of Liberal Arts Douglas Epperson were kind enough to grant me some time off from teaching so that I could complete this book. Department staff Susan Bratcher, Dee Lopez, and Cassandra Sherburne helped me in numerous ways practically every day, and I want to express my sincere appreciation for everything they have done and continue to do. Cal Poly's librarians—Sharon Andresen (Reserves), Brett Bodemer (Liberal Arts), Judy Drake (Circulation), Jan Kline and Karen Beaton (Acquisitions), Karen Lauritsen (Communications), Heather Lucio (Current Periodicals), and Michael Price (Information Technology)—never seemed to tire of giving me research aid, checking out books and journals to me, tracking down mounds of materials through interlibrary loan, and providing whatever other kinds of help I needed. They are wonderful.

Anyone doing scholarly work on Palahniuk owes an immense debt to Dennis Widmyer, whose website The Cult (chuckpalahniuk.net) has, ever since 1999, been the main source for all the latest information regarding this author. Thank you, Dennis, for the extraordinary service you have provided. Francisco Collado-Rodríguez, Cynthia Kuhn, Lance Rubin, Jeffrey A. Sartain, and Read Mercer Schuchardt also deserve credit for having edited the first scholarly books devoted to Palahniuk. I have learned a great deal from their essay collections.

My sister, Kathryn O'Brien, is an avid Palahniuk fan. Her enthusiasm has helped to motivate me in the writing of this book. My parents, Phyllis and Donald Keesey, gave me needed encouragement at just the right time. For this, as for so much else, I am profoundly grateful to them. And my wife, Helen Bailey, whose passionate support of me has been unwavering, can never be sufficiently acknowledged. What Palahniuk recently said about him and his longtime partner in an interview with Kevin Perry is true of me and mine as well: "I'm just glad that my partner is really good at letting me be obsessed with what I'm obsessed about. I'm really blessed."

CHAPTER 1

Understanding Chuck Palahniuk

Charles Michael Palahniuk was born in the small desert town of Pasco, Washington, on February 21, 1962. In *Invisible Monsters,* Palahniuk writes that "the future ended in 1962 at the Seattle World's Fair."[1] This event saw the construction of the Monorail and the Space Needle, bold projections of a future that never came to pass, but that instead gave way in subsequent years to a world "fixated on pollution, disease, war and hardship," according to Palahniuk. He used 1962 to "suggest that 'tipping point' in people's lives, when they become disillusioned with their dreams."[2] Only an author attuned to the dark side of things would trace the end of the future back to the year of his birth.

As the second of four children, Palahniuk grew up with his siblings in a mobile home when the family relocated to the nearby town of Burbank, Washington. As he put it, "My own background runs to trailer houses situated on gravel roads accessed by dented pick-up trucks."[3] He described their trailer as "sandwiched between a state prison and a nuclear reactor."[4] His father worked as a railroad brakeman, and Palahniuk recalls his dad taking him and the other kids to derailed train cars in order to scavenge for food among the wreckage. Other childhood memories include playing hide-and-seek in fogs of pesticide sprayed on crops, handling paper bills from a floor safe contaminated by waste water from overflowing toilets, and eating meals while wondering whether nuclear radiation had polluted the food chain.

During his first three years at school, Palahniuk thought it strange that classroom clocks were hung so high on the wall that you could not read the time. It was only when he was finally able to get his first pair of glasses that the world came into clearer focus. Perhaps this also accounts for why he did not learn to read or write until age eight or nine. "I was filled with terror that I was going to be left behind" the other kids, he said,[5] but after finally having some success, "I was so relieved and filled with joy that I decided I'd make my life's career out of this hard-won skill."[6] Still, he recalls the "heartbreaking" moment when he heard that everyone in school, including kids he thought were his friends, had been spreading the rumor that he was "retarded."[7]

When he was eleven or twelve, teachers decided that he needed to spend time in the gym lifting weights because he just was not "*boy* enough." As a result, he was given "special coaching" on how to bulk up and be more "*masculine*."[8] Certainly, to hear Palahniuk describe it, his educational environment was not one where differences were tolerated or where vulnerable students were protected: "my high school was akin to a prison, rife with date rape (before it was [called] date rape) and queer bashing (before it was [called] queer bashing). Students just took their lumps and held their tongues. And if you complained the principal swatted you with a wooden paddle."[9]

Home life, too, was far from easy. Palahniuk's mother was not happy about the fact that his father was often away, including spending significant time at the local bar. When his parents were both at home, they quarreled a lot, despite their children's often desperate attempts to keep the peace. "To interrupt a loud fight between my parents," Palahniuk recalled, "I once jumped on a needle that was sticking out of the carpet. When I hopped, bleeding, into the kitchen, the shouting ended like magic."[10] But the fighting did not stop for long—his parents eventually divorced, when he was only thirteen. Palahniuk has since suffered from years of anxiety and insomnia, which he traces back to his time spent as a child in the midst of an acrimonious marriage. At age eighteen, he did learn a family secret that he said has helped him to understand that his father never had a model for how to be in a happy marriage: Palahniuk found out that his paternal grandfather had killed his grandmother and then himself when Palahniuk's father was still a young boy.

Following high school, Palahniuk left home to attend the University of Oregon, where, inspired by Woodward and Bernstein's Watergate reporting, he earned a journalism degree in the hope of making a career in that field. However, saddled with student loan debt and unable to find a reporting job that would pay him more than a pittance, he was compelled to quit journalism and seek other employment. The position he got, which he later characterized as "the worst job you could possibly imagine,"[11] was as a mechanic at a diesel-truck manufacturing plant in Portland. The work was dirty and dangerous, as it involved lying on his back for eight hours every day installing drivelines on trucks as they moved down the assembly line. Fortunately, after several years of this, he was able to vary the work by also writing technical repair manuals. Palahniuk spent thirteen years, from age twenty-two to thirty-five, working at Freightliner Trucks, feeling stuck there, and getting increasingly angry, which he expressed by getting into brawls—one of which became the inspiration for *Fight Club.*

It is fair to say, then, that Palahniuk knows something about blue-collar work and the kind of rage that can build up in those who feel trapped in such jobs. He connects with working-class people, many of them young, who do not usually read fiction—and who may not regularly read anything at all. His writing features characters, situations, and language with which they can identify. Because it speaks to them and expresses some of the things they would say about their lives if they could, they become his avid fans, with some of them finding value in reading for the very first time. When Palahniuk attended a personal development seminar in 1988 and was asked to state "some huge impossible thing" that he would devote the rest of his life to, he said, "I want to write books that bring people back to reading."[12]

Palahniuk's books sell briskly, regularly making the *New York Times* best-seller list. If he is an author with a cult following, that cult is large. And yet, despite being a fan favorite, he is hardly a critical darling. Newspaper, magazine, and web reviewers often pan his fiction. The volume and vehemence of these negative reviews suggest that some readers still struggle with impediments to enjoying this writer's works. Nevertheless, the success of the 1999 *Fight Club* movie sent sales of Palahniuk's novel skyrocketing. Suddenly, the first-time author was famous—and widely influential. Impromptu fight clubs sprang up around the country, drawing participants as varied as high-school teens in Texas, Silicon Valley techies, and Mormon students at Brigham Young University. The phenomenon was parodied in the tea-party mêlée of "Jane Austen's Fight Club," a YouTube video that went viral. Palahniuk himself received numerous snapshots of fans proudly posing with bruised faces and was regularly asked by readers, "Can I hit you really, really hard?"[13] *Fight Club*–inspired food pranks reportedly invaded the culinary world; Gucci and Versace had runway stars sporting black eyes and adorned with razor blades modeling the "fight club look";[14] and the rules of fight club became a pervasive cultural meme, adopted and adapted everywhere. The impact on society was hotly debated by cultural commentators, perhaps most intelligently by Henry A. Giroux—for the prosecution—in "*Fight Club,* Patriarchy, and the Politics of Masculine Violence,"[15] followed by—speaking for the defense—Gary Crowdus in "Getting Exercised over *Fight Club*"[16] and Susan Faludi in "It's *Thelma and Louise* for Guys."[17]

A writer whose first book achieves great fame will always live in the shadow of that early success. Palahniuk has never abjured or disparaged his neophyte novel. Over the years he has happily signed fan copies of it, appeared on numerous panels to discuss it, and fielded countless interview questions about its inception and impact. And, despite having resolutely maintained that he would "never write a sequel,"[18] he has recently relented and done exactly that, although it should be noted that *Fight Club 2* does take a somewhat different form, that of a graphic novel with chapters published serially by Dark Horse Comics. Yet the phenomenon of his first book's fame has sometimes seemed to loom over him. Asked once whether he ever worries about being "labeled the *Fight Club* guy forever," Palahniuk replied, "Too late. I'm already that '*Fight Club* guy.' Now my mission is to be that 'anything else' guy."[19] Perhaps most gallingly, critics have tended to make invidious comparisons, viewing Palahniuk's later works as inferior when measured against their famous predecessor. "As the author of *Fight Club,* Mr. Palahniuk legitimately and brilliantly shocked readers," writes Janet Maslin in the *New York Times,* "but he also opened the floodgates for wretched excess of a less inspired kind," which is the way she characterizes his book *Haunted.*[20] Field Maloney of the *New York Times Book Review* believes that, while "*Fight Club* had a cold stylish gleam," the gleam is gone from Palahniuk's *Rant* and "all that's left is shock as shtick."[21] Reviewing *Doomed,* Tim Martin of the British *Telegraph* says that Palahniuk's "early work crackled with evil humour," but "his later novels shuffle weakly between leitmotifs of unpleasantness."[22]

Readers who come to Palahniuk's fiction out of enthusiasm for *Fight Club* will find many features of that great novel carried on in his later work, but in order to appreciate all that this author has to offer, they must get beyond just expecting more of the same. Over the nearly twenty years since the appearance of that novel, Palahniuk has explored a remarkably diverse range of subjects and styles, challenging readers to grow and change with him. In addition to male narrators (*Fight Club, Survivor, Choke, Lullaby, Pygmy*), his books have featured female storytellers (*Invisible Monsters, Diary, Tell-All, Damned, Doomed*) as well as multiple points of view (*Haunted, Rant, Snuff*). He has ventured into—or been influenced by—a variety of genres, including the road novel (*Invisible Monsters*), horror (*Lullaby, Diary, Haunted*), science fiction (*Rant*), pornography (*Snuff*), chick lit (*Beautiful You*), Hollywood memoir (*Tell-All*), the young adult novel (*Damned*), and the religious journey to redemption (*Doomed*). Palahniuk's fiction has taken such innovative forms as an in-flight "black box" tape recording (*Survivor*), a personal inventory for a twelve-step program (*Choke*), a diary kept for a coma victim (*Diary*), an undercover agent's dispatches to the homeland (*Pygmy*), stories read aloud at a writers' retreat (*Haunted*), a star biography (*Tell-All*), and a spiritual confession (*Doomed*). *Fight Club* was indeed a monumental work—it deserves and receives the most extended discussion in this book—but readers who can make themselves receptive to Palahniuk's other novels will find much of interest and excitement there.

Some reviewers have shown an unfortunate tendency to mock a certain segment of Palahniuk's readership, claiming that he writes "angry young man" fiction fit only for immature teens and twenty-somethings. Such critics describe Palahniuk's work as "raw but insular, angry but self-coddling, like a teenager's moods."[23] "Whatever emotional depth he achieves is undercut by his seemingly incurable adolescent streak."[24] Palahniuk's books are said to "traffic in the half-baked nihilism of a stoned high school student."[25] They exhibit an "adolescent urge to shock" that is "facile,"[26] and they express outrage in "bumper-sticker-like rallying cries" that are "catnip to preadults."[27] Palahniuk's readers are subjected to condescension and mockery by critics, who describe them as an "army of disenfranchised Everymen,"[28] "teenagers and the sort of young man whose disaffection springs from hazy origins,"[29] or "fan boys, wild with rage, choked by love and loyalty (like Ayn Rand devotees but with tattoos and tire irons)."[30] Palahniuk himself wrote an angry reply to one such review, calling it "cruel and mean-spirited"[31] for "ridiculing the people who read my books, characterizing them as stupid, or oafish."[32] Christopher Tayler of the UK *Guardian* may well be right in saying that "Palahniuk is one of those writers who get punished by critics for making them feel embarrassed about the eagerness with which their adolescent selves might have joined the writer's fan base."[33]

Granted, some fans may be angsty adolescents with an overblown sense of life's woes and their own causes for grievance, and their zealous devotion to the author may go to alarming extremes. One young man burned his hand with lye in imitation of *Fight Club*'s Tyler Durden, claiming, "This makes me feel like I'm connecting with what I love. I have passion."[34] It is easy to ridicule such hyperbolic gestures, but who is to say that this man has not experienced real suffering in his life, sufficient for him to seek an outlet in Palahniuk's books? "He's been a big influence in my life for the last couple years," the man said, adding that the author's work had "helped me a lot": "It wasn't just about violence, it was about how you can feel so alone in life and so abandoned and rejected by everything that you have to resort to violence to feel real."[35] This is not an unsophisticated interpretation of *Fight Club,* and if reading that book has allowed this young man to comprehend—to understand and contain—his negative feelings by finding them expressed in fiction, then perhaps the connection between Palahniuk and his fans is deeper and more meaningful than critics have supposed. A number of these fans are blue-collar workers living hardscrabble lives, or others, like young people, who struggle to make sense of and find solace in a world where they feel relatively powerless. Could it be that Palahniuk's connection with them is one of class solidarity, that his work serves to express feelings in them that might otherwise find a more destructive outlet? It is interesting to note that, according to Palahniuk, "Mr. Olsen in the fifth grade made me want to be a writer. He said, 'Chuck, you do this really well. And this is much better than setting fires, so keep it up.'"[36]

Palahniuk *is* shocking—a fact that certain reviewers, disdaining this tactic and the readers who enjoy it, fixate on and cannot seem to get past. It becomes literally all that these critics can see. For them, Palahniuk "revels in the gross,"[37] turning out "indiscriminately spewed nastiness."[38] His "themes range . . . from the queasily gynecological to the queasily gastrointestinal."[39] We are told that "every five pages or so the author of these novels will describe something as smelling like shit or piss."[40] His work is "crap . . . flung flesh against the wall and obsessively smeared by a deeply troubled fellow."[41] It is "the verbal equivalent to chunks of infantile regurgitate."[42] And so all of Palahniuk's writing gets reduced to an "urge to become ever more offensive to hold an audience's attention,"[43] "prodding . . . in book after book at the disgust reflexes of bored teens."[44]

This attitude seems unduly derogatory and dismissive. A more open-minded approach might be to consider whether the emphasis on the physical in Palahniuk's fiction could serve some purpose beyond mere sensationalism to draw in blasé readers. In 1990, while he was still working at Freightliner Trucks, Palahniuk began to attend a writers' workshop run by Tom Spanbauer. One of the techniques taught there, called "going on the body," involves conveying a character's experience by describing it in very physical terms so that the reader can feel what the character feels and thus form an even closer identification with him or her. "That's why all my stories tend to involve sex, or violence, or drugs, or illness, or accidents," Palahniuk explains, "because they are strong visceral events that generate a sympathetic engagement from the reader."[45] Palahniuk might as well be addressing his critics directly when he notes that "intellectual culture seems to separate high art from low art. Low art is horror or pornography or anything that has a physical component to it. . . . High art is people driving in Volvos and talking a lot. I just don't want to keep those things separate. I think you can use visceral physical experiences to illustrate larger ideas, whether they're emotional or spiritual."[46] Making his fiction bracingly physical is part of Palahniuk's strategy to attract people who don't normally read because they find that most books don't affect them on a gut level. As he has said, "so many of the books I was required to read that deadened me to reading in school were books that were either very intellectual or they were very emotional. . . . But they were rarely ever visceral."[47]

Some other aspects of Palahniuk's fiction that have appeal for casual readers convey a sense of his aesthetic. At least prior to *Pygmy,* his work has tended to follow the tenets of "minimalism" as he learned them in Spanbauer's workshop. Befitting their emphasis on the physical, Palahniuk's novels have fast-moving plots with lots of action. The novels—novellas really, often with one-word titles—are propelled by a series of short scenes; it is not unusual for there to be one-sentence paragraphs. What characters do is reported in the present tense using concrete sensory detail, while overt statements about their motives or feelings tend to be avoided. Also eschewed are moral pronouncements by any omniscient third person, which "allows room for the reader to make his or her judgments," according to Palahniuk.[48] Considering his work to be part of an "oral storytelling tradition,"[49] Palahniuk has his narrators tell their tales in an informal, conversational style. As they speak, his narrators can switch unpredictably among first ("I"), second ("you"), and third ("he" or "she") persons, and their minds can jump suddenly from one thought, place, or time to another. Rather than provide explanatory links bridging these gaps, Palahniuk—inspired by dynamic film editing—will often "just put one detail next to another" and "allow the reader to decide what the relationship is."[50]

This is not to say that his novels are lacking in coherence or characterization. A central tenet of minimalist fiction is that it must be unified around a limited number of main themes, key characters, and symbolic objects. The themes, known as "horses" because they carry the reader from the start to the end of the story, are repeated throughout the narrative, each time being illustrated in a different way. In *Choke,* for example, the theme that "Things are NOT what they appear" is illustrated by the "coded security announcements," the "symptoms of disease," and the "female protagonist."[51] Objects that reappear, accruing more meaning as they do, include Brandy's hands in *Invisible Monsters,* Helen's suit in *Lullaby,* and Misty's brooch in *Diary.* And Palahniuk has become famous for his repeated phrases or "choruses," such as "The first rule about fight club is . . . ," "Give me [X]. Give me [Y]. Flash!" (*Invisible Monsters*), and "What Would Jesus NOT do?" (*Choke*).

Characterization is achieved by having narrators reveal themselves through the particular words they use to describe the world. Palahniuk employs a specific technique known as "burnt tongue," wherein verbal mistakes not only make what a character says less clichéd and more memorable, they also speak volumes about his or her personality and perspective. An extreme example of this would be Pygmy, whose unromantic outlook is shown when he describes a school dance in which "Females flaunt dermis and hair to depict viable vessel for impregnate."[52] More generally, Palahniuk often develops his characters by having them provide informational tidbits or "factoids" that convey the kinds of people they are. Tyler's bomb recipes in *Fight Club*, Tender's cleaning tips in *Survivor*, Victor's history lessons in *Choke*, and Cassie's porn lore in *Snuff* are more than just bizarre and obscure facts; they also tell us about the types of persons whose perspectives are formed by such knowledge, those who view the world through its filter. As a way of learning about people and gathering the "factoids" he needs to create his characters, Palahniuk not only does extensive library research, he also explores the world in real-life settings, such as attending support groups (*Fight Club, Choke*), conferring with transsexuals about surgery (*Invisible Monsters*), going on the Big Car Hunt at Burning Man (*Rant*), and observing what happens behind the scenes on porn sets (*Snuff*). By engaging in such investigations, Palahniuk has perhaps fulfilled some of his original ambition to become a journalist. He once said, "Some writers research in order to write. I write in order to research topics that interest me."[53]

As another strategy for gathering information and inspiration for his work, Palahniuk also practices what he calls "crowd-seeding": at parties and other public events, he will plant the germ of an idea and then use people's responses to help him develop it. "I request information and they provide me with anecdotes from their lives," Palahniuk says.[54] "My job is to find a shared pattern in the experiences of these disparate people and quilt their anecdotes into something larger"—a coherent and meaningful novel.[55] Beyond containing factual details, Palahniuk's novels frequently borrow from nonfiction forms. These not only add a variety of different "textures" to his work, they also help to ground his often outlandish tales in reality. Likening them to the documentary newsreel in *Citizen Kane* and the found video footage in *The Blair Witch Project*, Palahniuk has said that the nonfiction forms he adopts—whether big (diaries, biographies, official reports) or small (graffiti, epitaphs, product warnings, political slogans, technical jargon)—serve to make his fiction more believable and that this added credibility is part of what attracts those who do not normally read novels. In sum, these people are drawn by the physicality, immediacy, informality, and factuality of his fiction.

Fight Club's Tyler Durden is seductive, particularly as incarnated by Brad Pitt in the movie, and his actions and attitudes do become increasingly destructive. Perhaps this is the origin of the widespread critical belief that Palahniuk himself is "a dime-store nihilist"[56] and that his books exhibit "cheap, high-school nihilism"[57] or exude "pop-nihilist bile."[58] His work is accused of being unremittingly and pointlessly negative, "angrier than it needs to be"[59] and "as savagely glib as what it derides,"[60] "like reading a long e-mail message about someone's senseless, if inventive, nightmare."[61] For some critics, Palahniuk's fiction expresses nothing but loathing—a charge made against him again and again: "Palahniuk the rageaholic is now so furious he's reached the point where it's hard to know who he hates most: his readers, his characters or himself."[62] "Revulsion is expressed indiscriminately: Palahniuk is contemptuous of everything and everybody! Including, I suspect, us."[63] "If one is to believe Palahniuk's version of the world, there is nothing worth saving. . . . Everything is damned. Palahniuk's is a deeply cynical outlook."[64]

This characterization of Palahniuk as a complete pessimist prevents critics from seeing that he is actually a satirist with specific targets for opprobrium. While it is true that he is not always overtly disapproving, often leaving room for readers to make their own judgments, nevertheless it is not terribly difficult to determine which social ills are the objects of his ire. Palahniuk takes precise aim at such targets as corporations and wealthy elites that put profit before human life (*Fight Club, Diary*), beauty and sex industries that trap women and men within gender norms (*Invisible Monsters, Snuff*), religious indoctrination (*Survivor*) and patriotic propaganda (*Pygmy*), along with media saturation of our minds (*Lullaby*). Palahniuk exposes the harmful effect of haunting family legacies (*Choke, Rant*), the guilt induced by narrow notions of sin (*Damned, Doomed*), and the destructive impact of idealizing myths (*Tell-All*). He reveals the damage done when spirit is reduced to flesh (*Haunted*) and when sexuality is commodified (*Snuff, Beautiful You*).

The fact that Palahniuk's narrators and main protagonists are not immune to his satire may be another reason that critics accuse him of nihilism and misanthropy. "All the characters," one reviewer lamented, "are mired in self-loathing."[65] But when Palahniuk presents faulty and compromised characters, it is not in order to denounce and distance them from the rest of society; instead, it is to show that they are very much *like us* in their flawed humanity. As he describes his strategy for creating narrators, "you risk revealing something that makes you look bad. You allow yourself to become the fool instead of the hero. . . . You admit your failures and weakness, and doing so lets your reader admit and accept their own."[66] Palahniuk often likens fiction writing to therapy, and he compares his narrators to those confessing their flaws to a support group: "They're like idiot heroes, or fool heroes, in that if somebody steps forward and plays the fool they create a place where everybody can just relax and not have to worry about looking good. Which is what support groups are really about: . . . you can look like an asshole and they still accept you."[67] Most Palahniuk protagonists spend the first part of each book as evaders or outright liars, hiding unflattering truths from others or from themselves, but eventually they "overuse their coping mechanisms to the point where they break down"[68] and their "big lie can fall apart."[69] This is the moment when they must confess the truth about themselves. Because the novels frequently turn on these moments of self-revelation, those who wish to preserve the surprise are advised to read the novels before turning to the chapters in this book.

A protagonist's honest admission of frailty and fault will often lead to forgiveness by a loved one and reconciliation with society. Palahniuk has repeatedly denied that he is a nihilist, insisting that he is a romantic at heart and a believer in community. As he sees it, no matter what particular tale he tells, the "story is always a romance, always [about] someone being delivered from isolation back into community and ultimately back into a committed relationship."[70] Consider how many of his novels end with the lead character, often after having confessed to a big lie, pairing up with a beloved. An abbreviated list might include Shannon and her groom in *Invisible Monsters Remix,* Victor and Paige in *Choke,* Streator and Helen in *Lullaby,* and Sheila and Darin in *Snuff.* Also, though their conclusions are more ambiguous or otherwise problematic, there are the loving relationships between "Jack" and Marla in *Fight Club,* Tender and Fertility in *Survivor,* Rant and Echo in *Rant,* and Pygmy and his host "sister" in *Pygmy.*

When it comes to community, it is worth noting that Palahniuk is not just interested in attacking existing institutions; he also wants to explore possibilities for improved social arrangements. An early and pervasive influence on Palahniuk was cultural anthropologist Victor Turner with his ideas about social change. Turner described society as "a structured, differentiated, and often hierarchical system of politico-legal-economic positions with many types of evaluation, separating men in terms of 'more' or 'less.'" However, in its transitional or "liminal" phase when society is undergoing significant change, it becomes "an unstructured or rudimentarily structured and relatively undifferentiated *comitatus,* community, or even communion of equal individuals."[71] Although these individuals may eventually become fixed in another hierarchy when society settles into a new form of stability, for the time being they enjoy a relative freedom and equality: "Liminal entities are neither here nor there; they are betwixt and between the positions assigned by law, custom, convention, and ceremonial. . . . Among themselves, [they] tend to develop an intense comradeship and egalitarianism."[72]

Palahniuk has said, "Almost all of my books depict the kind of social experiments that Victor Turner described in his work"[73]—"people experimenting with different identities and social models in a short-term way" in the hope that they can "break through to something authentic."[74] Think of the fistfights in *Fight Club*; *Rant*'s demolition derbies ("*Fight Club* with cars");[75] the road trips in *Invisible Monsters, Survivor,* and *Lullaby*; the writers' retreat in *Haunted*; *Snuff*'s porn movie set; and the teen hell in *Damned.* Of course, not all these attempts to break away from existing conventions to create a more perfect society are successful—*Haunted*'s cannibalism marks a memorable failure—but in a number of cases the social experiments conducted by Palahniuk's characters do lead them to a "dysfunctional, unpleasant, chaotic, but ultimately more fulfilling community."[76]

Palahniuk tends to provoke strong reader reactions. For every reviewer who thinks of him as "dimwitted" and "functionally illiterate"[77]—indeed, as "a writer who does not know how to write"[78]—there is another whose praise goes to the opposite extreme, describing Palahniuk's works as "utterly original,"[79] "from so far left field they might as well be lobbed from outer space," and claiming "his style . . . breaks all rules and conventions, like he never even learned them."[80] But those who laud him as an incomparable genius—or idiot savant—and those who brand him an illiterate fool both miss the opportunity to understand him as working within a larger literary context.

Given the sparseness of his writing style, it should come as no surprise that Palahniuk has expressed a kinship with the pared-down fiction of Ernest Hemingway and John Steinbeck—an emphasis on surface description and an absence of emotive adjectives that would become known as minimalism, influencing later writers, most notably Raymond Carver. Carver's editor, Gordon Lish, taught Tom Spanbauer, who in turn became Palahniuk's mentor. Carver was a master of the short form, and it is worth noting that most of the writers with the greatest impact on Palahniuk are best known as authors of stories, novellas, or essays. Foremost among these is Palahniuk's favorite writer, Amy Hempel, whose *Collected Stories* he has praised for the way their "distanced" and "fracture[d]" presentation of factual details builds up a cumulative emotional power:[81] "It's just a simple list of facts presented in the first person, but somehow it adds up to more than the sum of its parts. Most of the facts are funny as hell, but at the last moment, when you're disarmed by laughter, it breaks your heart."[82] Other short-story writers with the sharply observed details, dark humor, and earned emotion that Palahniuk admires include Peter Christopher (*Campfires of the Dead*), Junot Diaz (*Drown*), Bret Easton Ellis (*The Informers*), A. M. Homes (*The Safety of Objects*), Tama Janowitz (*Slaves of New York*), Denis Johnson (*Jesus' Son*), Thom Jones (*The Pugilist at Rest*), and Mark Richard (*The Ice at the Bottom of the World*). Essayists who have influenced him with their outspoken courage and sardonic wit include Joan Didion (*Slouching Towards Bethlehem*), Nora Ephron (*Crazy Salad*), David Sedaris (*Barrel Fever*), and Joy Williams (*Ill Nature*).

Palahniuk has also found inspiration in authors who are more recognizably genre-specific. Some readers may be surprised to learn that, when he was asked to name "The Book That Changed My Life," Palahniuk said it was the Ellery Queen mysteries, which he has praised for teaching him that "most books . . .

work as a series of withholds and reveals."[83] In fact, almost all Palahniuk novels have strong mystery elements, for he loves "plot twists and hidden back stories and big reveals."[84] Such traits are often features of horror fiction as well, and ever since his first—unpublished—book, which he described as "a seven hundred page, fake Stephen King novel,"[85] Palahniuk's works have borrowed elements from the horror genre such as haunted houses, grotesque bodies, and gruesome deaths. The key influences here, aside from King (particularly *Night Shift* and *Carrie*), have been the stories and novellas of Edgar Allan Poe, Shirley Jackson ("The Lottery" and *The Haunting of Hill House*), Ira Levin (*Rosemary's Baby* and *The Stepford Wives*), and Clive Barker (*The Books of Blood*). Science fiction has also had some impact on Palahniuk's work, especially *Rant,* as informed by his reading of Ray Bradbury (*The Martian Chronicles*) and the hallucinatory, time-twisting tales of Philip K. Dick.

Palahniuk's protagonists are social misfits and protesters, and in characterizing them he has often drawn upon his own eclectic "tradition" of literary rebels, most notably Jay Gatsby (*The Great Gatsby*), Scarlett O'Hara (*Gone with the Wind*), Sally Bowles (*Goodbye to Berlin*), Holly Golightly (*Breakfast at Tiffany's*), Randle Patrick McMurphy (*One Flew Over the Cuckoo's Nest*), and Neely O'Hara (*Valley of the Dolls*). At least partly at the suggestion of his editor, Palahniuk has sometimes linked his works to more contemporary novels of rebellion grouped together under the heading of "transgressional" or "transgressive" writing, which he has defined as "fiction in which characters misbehave and act badly, commit crimes or pranks, as a way of either feeling alive or as political acts of civil disobedience."[86] In this category, he includes such novels as Edward Abbey's *The Monkey Wrench Gang,* Katherine Dunn's *Geek Love,* Bret Easton Ellis's *American Psycho,* and Irvine Welsh's *Trainspotting.* As forerunners of this kind of defiant or insurrectionary fiction, Palahniuk has sometimes cited Mark Twain (*The Adventures of Huckleberry Finn*), Nathanael West (*The Day of the Locust*), George Orwell (*1984*), and Kurt Vonnegut Jr. (*Slaughterhouse-Five*), and among its current practitioners he has mentioned Michel Houellebecq (*Platform*) and Lidia Yuknavitch (*Dora*).

Recent scholarship has also made progress toward situating Palahniuk's fiction within some revealing contexts. Robin Mookerjee sees Palahniuk as continuing in the venerable tradition of social satire but making it more transgressive by refusing to specify which behavior is bad or to prescribe solutions for society's ills: "Transgressive satirists treat flashpoint subjects without taking any kind of moral stand and treat bizarre behavior as if it were absolutely normal. Further, they maintain a sort of authorial anonymity that makes it difficult to extract some semblance of intent from the work to clarify its meaning as a gesture."[87] Kathryn Hume places Palahniuk's work alongside other "aggressive fiction" that "tramples reader sensibilities" and "offends and upsets willfully and deliberately," but like Mookerjee, she sees this writing's offensive nature as having a satiric purpose: "political despair aimed at America is important for motivating this drive to bewilder and nauseate the reader. . . . Whereas conventional fiction reinforces cultural norms, this fiction tends to consider those norms evil or idiotic and works to undercut the reader complacence that rests on those common beliefs."[88] Both scholars note that one of the most potent weapons of satire is the grotesque or "monstrous" body, one whose unruly corporeality defies repressive rules and regulations ("carnal imagery as a reminder of visceral reality")[89] and upsets society's rigid order: "A reader harboring revolutionary sentiments might identify with the . . . chaotic set of values and welcome the horrible [grotesque body] if it meant destroying some aspect of the decorous world."[90] Palahniuk frequently uses the grotesque or "monstrous" body as a satiric attack on social norms, whether it be Jack's pummeled face in *Fight Club,* Shannon's mutilated visage in *Invisible Monsters,* Cassandra's wasted body in *Haunted,* or Rant's rabid flesh in *Rant.*

Disfigured and deformed bodies also feature prominently in horror, and given Palahniuk's affinity with this genre, his fiction could certainly be read within the context of the horror or Gothic tradition, which, as Catherine Spooner notes, often deals with "bodies that are modified, grotesque or diseased" and "the construction of peoples or individuals as monstrous or 'other.'"[91] However, Palahniuk's novels should be understood as belonging to a particular strand within the gothic, an increasingly popular trend toward embracing rather than abhorring rebellion and transgression. According to Fred Botting, "Where the restoration of symbolic, normative boundaries was celebrated in the violent climaxes to older tales of terror, monstrous figures are now less often terrifying objects of animosity expelled in the return to social and symbolic equilibrium. Instead, they retain a fascinating, attractive appeal: no longer objects of hate or fear, monstrous others become sites of identification, sympathy, desire, and self-recognition."[92] Indeed, in Palahniuk's work, "monstrous" characters are the externalized expression of *our* anger and suffering. Rather than abjuring the "monstrous" as "other," readers are invited to feel an almost physical compassion for Tender's sagging flesh (*Survivor*), Streator's bleeding foot (*Lullaby*), Misty's pierced skin (*Diary*), Katherine's "gouged" face (*Tell-All*), and Madison's "predecomposed" body (*Doomed*).

It is not only these literary traditions that have informed and inspired Palahniuk's fiction; there are significant cinematic and musical influences as well. His favorite films hail from that revolutionary period of the late 1960s and early 1970s that saw such unlikely heroes as the rebels played by Jane Fonda in *They Shoot Horses, Don't They?* and *Klute,* along with the outlaw lovers in *The*

Graduate and *Harold and Maude*. When it comes to music, Palahniuk has said that "the punk esthetic shaped my work: Start loud, run short, end abruptly."[93] Punk, industrial rock, and other edgy, confrontational styles tend to be the major influences, such as the music of Billy Idol (*Pygmy*) and Nine Inch Nails (*Fight Club* and *Lullaby*). To get into the right mood to create his damaged and sometimes dangerous characters, Palahniuk will often listen to the same song on repeat while he is writing. These have included Radiohead's "Creep" for *Choke*, Depeche Mode's "Little 15" for *Diary*, and Bauhaus's "Bela Lugosi's Dead" for *Haunted*.

And so, while Palahniuk's voice *is* distinctive, it is not "utterly original."[94] He is surrounded by influential peers and predecessors whose work he takes in and transforms to make his own innovative contribution to literary tradition. Perhaps the fans who read him so zealously will be inspired to try some works by other authors too, in which case he will have achieved his goal to "get a generation of people that have not been involved in books involved in reading."[95]

CHAPTER 2

The Struggle for Identity

Fight Club, Invisible Monsters, Survivor, Choke

Describing his first four books as being about "the struggle to find personal identity,"[1] Palahniuk has located his works alongside Henry James's *The Bostonians,* F. Scott Fitzgerald's *The Great Gatsby,* and Truman Capote's *Breakfast at Tiffany's* in dealing with "the central, most American literary theme," which is "the invention of self." "It's such an American genre," the author has said, "this whole idea of reinventing and creating your self based on your dream, or how you perceive yourself to be, or not to be." Each of the novels in Palahniuk's identity tetralogy marks an attempt to explore this theme from a different angle: "*Fight Club* is based on what you are not; *Invisible Monsters* was based on recreating yourself based on fashion and fantasy; *Survivor* was based on creating yourself in the face of immortality; and *Choke* was based on creating yourself out of a purpose, out of something you stake your life on, that you commit to."[2]

Although *Fight Club* is Palahniuk's first-published and best-known novel, *Invisible Monsters* was written beforehand, but it kept being rejected by the publishing houses as "too dark and too risky." So, in a gesture of defiance directed at the New York literary establishment, Palahniuk wrote *Fight Club,* making it "even darker and riskier and more offensive, all the things that they didn't want," figuring that "they wouldn't buy it, but at least they wouldn't forget it."[3] To his surprise, *Fight Club* was accepted for publication and appeared in 1996. But the book did not sell well, and most of the remaining copies of the novel were about to be pulped when David Fincher's film adaptation debuted in 1999. Even the film seemed as though it could fail—grosses fell sharply after its premiere weekend—but it gradually developed a significant cult following on video, generating interest in Palahniuk's novel and jump-starting his literary career. Owing to the popularity of the film, Palahniuk's *Fight Club* was reissued in paperback with a movie tie-in cover, and *Invisible Monsters* and *Survivor*—manuscripts that had been previously rejected—were both speedily published.

If the *Fight Club* movie helped to sell the book, it is fair to say that the film's success owed a great deal to the novel. Originally, screenwriter Jim Uhls had written the script without the narrator's voice-over from the novel, but director Fincher protested, "It was like taking the voice out of Dashiell Hammett":[4] "The strongest thing this film has going for it is Chuck's voice."[5] The narrator (in both the book and the film) is unnamed, because he is Everyman and because he is suffering an identity crisis, unsure of who he really is. For the sake of convenience, I follow the critical convention, which has grown up around the film, of calling the narrator "Jack." In addition, while the focus of my analysis is the novel, I occasionally quote critics of the film when their insights seem equally relevant to Palahniuk's work. The film's main divergence from the novel occurs in the ending.

Fight Club

Jack, a white-collar worker, is afflicted with insomnia, wherein "everything becomes an out-of-body experience": "you can't touch anything and nothing can touch you."[6] Jack's job distances him from his own feelings about others' deaths. He is employed by a major car company as a recall coordinator, reducing fatalities to an abstract formula to determine how many lives lost are worth the cost of recalling a defective car. Jack floats through the world like a ghost, oblivious to others' pain and suffering, and repressing his own guilt and rage over his complicity in such callousness. Jack's job anesthetizes him against a fear of mortality but in the process deprives him of all feelings, including those of sympathy for others and joy in life. In an effort to feel again, he feigns sickness and begins to attend support groups for the terminally ill. Palahniuk himself, while volunteering as an escort for persons with cancer and AIDS, "confronted" his "fear of dying"[7] and felt more deeply connected with others: "I saw that people open up in a different, very raw way when they're dealing with death. Around death you can have bold, cathartic experiences. We miss them in life."[8] At the same time, when support group members mistakenly assumed that he was one of them, Palahniuk began "feeling really guilty about being the healthy person sitting there—'The Tourist.'"[9] This gave him the idea for Jack: while others are being honest about their illness, he is lying. While the bonds they make with fellow sufferers can be genuine, his are weakened by falsehood. He is in the compromised position of seeking a real connection without a true willingness to commit to one, of perpetrating an "emotional scam" in order to "steal some humanity," as the author put it.[10]

Nevertheless, Jack does make a kind of connection with a character named Big Bob at a testicular cancer support group. Big Bob used to own a gym, have a barrel chest, and flex his muscles as a bodybuilder, an icon of masculinity. But, due to taking carcinogenic steroids, he had to have his testicles removed, and testosterone treatments have since caused his body to produce increased estrogen as a counterbalance, giving him large breasts. Big Bob cries because he feels emasculated and feminized. Jack cries, too, finding that the emotional outlet finally allows him to sleep, but since his body has not been transformed in the way the other man's has, why does Jack feel connected to him?

Big Bob is the physical manifestation of Jack's own psychological condition, for Jack feels feminized by his white-collar job and his consumer lifestyle. Jack may not have literally lost his balls, but he still feels unmanned. As Susan Faludi argued in her book *Stiffed,* "the economic transition from industry to service" or from blue to white collar, along with the shift "from production to consumption" or from building to buying things, "is symbolically a move from the traditional masculine to the traditional feminine." This shift has been "more traumatic for men than we realize":[11] "Where we once lived in a society in which men in particular participated by being useful in public life, we now are surrounded by a culture that encourages people to play almost no functional public roles, only decorative or consumer ones."[12] It is worth noting that Palahniuk has called *Fight Club* "the fictionalized version of *Stiffed*."[13]

In performing the duties for his job, Jack is either stuck in his office or crammed into seats on airplanes, disempowered or carried passively along, unable to show any manly initiative or expansiveness: "I wanted a way out of my tiny life. Single-serving butter and cramped airline seat role in the world" (173). His fear that luggage handlers might suspect him of carrying a vibrating dildo rather than an electric razor in his suitcase is a sign of how feminized he feels in his job for the company. Jack's role as consumer is experienced as equally emasculating. His tendency to curl up in his condo and browse shopping catalogs for commodities to fill it is described in terms of a mother bird making her nest and of a man not even able to masturbate properly: "I wasn't the only slave to my nesting instinct. The people I know who used to sit in the bathroom with pornography, now they sit in the bathroom with their IKEA furniture catalogue" (43).

In this postindustrial world, manhood itself has become a commodity, and men are expected to work out in order to display a "beautiful stock body" like a "cherry" car in a "dealer's showroom" (48): "The gyms you go to are crowded with guys trying to look like men, as if being a man means looking the way a sculptor or an art director says," but "even a soufflé looks pumped" (50). The reference to an empty and effeminate "soufflé" suggests that such male modeling, such masculine posing under the direction of another's gaze, is more feminizing than it is virile. Jack's gym workouts connect him with Big Bob's bodybuilder poses, where "pumped and shaved on stage" (21) he would enact for the judges a performance of masculinity, in the process making himself a slave to their commands and the "feminine" object of their gaze. Thus, even though Jack has not had his testicles removed like Big Bob, he nevertheless feels castrated by a society that has reduced manhood to something merely "ornamental," to use Faludi's word. "The ordinary man is no fool," she argues; "he knows he can't be Arnold Schwarzenegger. Nonetheless, the culture reshapes his most basic sense of manhood by telling him as much as it tells the celebrity . . . that manhood is displayed, not demonstrated.[14] . . . The aspects of this public 'femininity'—objectification, passivity, infantilization, pedestal-perching, and mirror-gazing—are the very ones that women have in modern times denounced as trivializing and humiliating qualities imposed on them. . . . No wonder men are in such agony."[15]

When Big Bob enfolds Jack within his large breasts, the two men cry and bond over their shared sense of loss—the former's physical and the latter's psychological emasculation. Jack finally being able to cry and sleep like a baby suggests that he finds a maternal comfort in the bodybuilder's arms. It is possible to see Big Bob as an ideal combination of masculine and feminine traits, of strength and sympathy. In Lauren M. E. Goodlad's view, "we can recognize Big Bob's castrated and tit-endowed body as pointing beyond the disabling antinomies of post-Enlightenment sex/gender."[16] She argues that, when Big Bob and Jack hug and cry at the testicular cancer support group called Remaining Men Together, they point the way toward becoming a new kind of man, one that is empowered *through* compassion. Goodlad refers to "the novel's most visionary response to masculine discontent: a vision in which Big Bob and the narrator paradoxically 'remain men together' by facing down difference as androgynous subjects, 'beyond division,' across an intersubjective ethic of care."[17] Palahniuk could be hinting that every individual needs an "androgynous" balance of masculine and feminine psychological traits, much as every body seeks a harmony between male and female hormones: "Raise the testosterone level too much, your body ups the estrogen to seek a balance" (17).

But as much as Jack is drawn to empathize with Big Bob, to recognize aspects of his own plight in the bodybuilder's suffering, he is equally repulsed by the other man's "femininity," regarding it as a threat to his own precarious masculinity. Big Bob's breasts may offer maternal succor, but in Jack's mind they are also "bitch tits" (17)—a derogatory term revealing Jack's misogynistic reaction to the androgynous other man as a freak. Similarly, Big Bob's openness about his feelings may invite Jack to build strength by sharing, but it raises fears that, if he lets his guard down and admits his own weaknesses, he will have no macho defense to protect himself: "Strangers with this kind of honesty make me go a big rubbery one" (21). As Andrew Steven Delfino reads this line, "the narrator says that to be emotionally open, holding nothing back, is to be soft, vulnerable, and impotent, rather than hard and phallic."[18] For Jack, Big Bob's hugging and weeping seem too passive, too much like surrendering to adversity and dissolving in tears. Moreover, there are aspects of group therapy that seem like an "unmanly" retreat from disease and death, such as the upbeat group names (Remaining Men Together), the euphemisms used for illnesses, and the guided meditations designed to help sufferers ignore pain. Some part of Jack feels that "real men" are not supposed to hug and cry, to share and meditate; instead, they are expected to fight.

Enter Tyler Durden, the hypermasculine counterpart to feminized Big Bob. Though eventually revealed to be a split-off portion of the narrator's own psyche, Tyler initially appears as Jack's opposite in every way. We recall Palahniuk's description of *Fight Club* as a search for identity, a reinvention of self, "based on what you are not."[19] Tyler is working-class while Jack is white collar; Tyler is hard while Jack is soft; Tyler is physically powerful and rebellious while Jack tends toward passive conformity. The underground fight clubs that Tyler creates, which then morph into the even more insurrectionary activities of Project Mayhem, seem to provide a way that "men can be men" again. "Through the fist-fight," writes Benjamin A. Brabon, "the postfeminized man of feeling is re-born as the masculinized man of action,"[20] and James R. Giles asserts, "The narrator's subconscious projects fight club with its ritualized system of male aggression and violence as a means of transcending the emasculation of his generation of American males."[21] Jack's search for identity via Tyler does indeed provide him with some of the traditional satisfactions of macho empowerment, but Palahniuk makes this search considerably more complex than might be indicated by an initial understanding of fight club and Project Mayhem merely as avenues for violent action.

During the day, Jack works at his white-collar job, but at night he and Tyler engage in bare-knuckle brawling with other willing young men. The idea for fight club came to Palahniuk when he got into a fistfight on a weekend camping trip and then found, upon returning to work, that people just pretended to ignore the awful contusions on his face: "For months, no one looked me in the bruised face, and I realized that you could do anything in your private life as long as you looked so terrible nobody would want to know about it."[22] For fight club members, the freedom to misbehave at night, to engage in unlawful fisticuffs, acts as a kind of safety valve, enabling them to endure their boring, servile jobs during the day. Similarly, when fight club becomes Project Mayhem and the men begin pulling pranks like pushing over a guy in a chemical toilet or disrupting a fashion show by throwing strawberry gelatin, these anarchic acts allow them to blow off steam on their off-hours before going back to business as usual.

Palahniuk based Project Mayhem on the Cacophony Society, a loosely organized group of pranksters which began in San Francisco and then spread all over the world. When Palahniuk was a member of the Portland branch, he participated in the Santa Rampage, wherein hundreds of people, identically dressed as Father Christmas, sang, drank, and disrupted traffic throughout the town. Again, though, despite the implicit protest against capitalism—the commercialization of Christmas—inherent in this event, nothing really revolutionary occurred; the pranksters returned to their regular jobs when the "Santarchy" was over. "People at Cacophony tended to have structured lives," Palahniuk noted. "The Society gave them a limited window of chaos—the chance to go insane for a few hours and then return to their normal existence."[23] One can see this "window of chaos" as simply enabling the continuance of the established social order, venting a little steam so that no one really explodes in rage to transform it. However, it is also possible to view these pranks more positively as symbolic or artistic statements of protest, as if people were *experimenting with ideas* for rebellion—much as Palahniuk does in his transgressive fictions—rather than engaging in actual revolutionary acts.

Among the first assignments that Tyler gives to the members of Project Mayhem is for them to "pick a fight, and lose—to lose really badly," as the author put it.[24] The goal is not only to empower others, showing them that they have more strength than they thought, but also to make the men realize that they can survive a beating; they do not have to be so afraid of injury or loss of face. Like Palahniuk after that fistfight, Jack shows up at work with a horribly battered face, defying company expectations regarding proper appearance. One of the things Palahniuk liked most about the members of the Cacophony Society—such as those drunk, rampaging Santas—was that they were not afraid to flout accepted standards of conduct: "Cacophony allowed you to step away from that and be an idiot, an idiot who looked really ridiculous and pathetic":[25] "They looked like they didn't care how they looked. Like they never went to the gym or counted calories."[26] Contrary to much of society's emphasis on "biceps" and "posing," Cacophony offered "an escape from the treadmill of always looking good and always looking good and always looking. . . ."[27] Caring less about how you look in others' eyes, refusing to conform in that way to social expectations, may not be revolutionary, but it could count as one small step toward independence.

Two of *Fight Club*'s most famous lines—"Maybe self-improvement isn't the answer" and "Maybe self-destruction is the answer"—have another sentence between them: "Tyler never knew his father" (49). If Jack's white-collar job and his gym-perfect body and his furniture-stuffed condo have left him feeling unfulfilled, then maybe destroying these, which means destroying his false hope in them, will lead to the solution. If Tyler's absent father and Jack's clueless father cannot provide them with direction in life, then perhaps, rather than needing a father to complete themselves, they can turn to each other and to other sons for help. One of Palahniuk's inspirations for *Fight Club* was "a Bill Moyer[s] television program about how street gangs were really young men raised without fathers, just trying to help one another become men."[28] In *The Sibling Society*—another inspiration for Palahniuk's novel—Robert Bly argues, "Sons who have a remote or absent father clearly can receive no modeling on how to deal appropriately with male anger." Bly believes that such sons tend to "radiate an aggression that is diffuse, nondirectional, inconsolable."[29]

Fight club channels that aggression so that it does not implode as suicide or explode as indiscriminately murderous violence, such as "doing God knows what with automatic weapons at school"; here Palahniuk is referring to the Columbine massacre of 1999. Fight club allows male rage to be "vented in a consensual" environment, providing a "structured, controlled way of just going nuts in a really safe situation."[30] Indeed, *fight club* is something of an oxymoron, like *safe violence* or *controlled insanity.* It is worth remembering that fight club has rules beyond the two specifying that you do not talk about it, which include the safeguard that you must quit fighting when your opponent says stop or goes limp. Despite its violence, fight club is not about dealing the killing blow but about male bonding—what Palahniuk calls "a new social model for men to share their lives."[31] Fight club is ideally about gaining self-confidence, if you are the victor, or building endurance, if you are beaten. It establishes mutually supportive connections among heretofore isolated and angry young men.

But violence, once it is unleashed, does not prove to be so easily controlled. One night at fight club, Jack gives another young man (Angel Face) such a severe beatdown that he has to be hospitalized. Rather than serving as an outlet for aggression, violence acts like an addictive drug, causing Jack to develop a "jones" for more and more, a need for "something bigger" to give him that "buzz." This is when Tyler takes things "up a notch" (123) and invents Project Mayhem, which begins as anarchic pranks but then escalates into military-style maneuvers that involve shooting people and blowing up buildings. In beating up Angel Face, Jack is motivated not by a need to build male camaraderie, but by a desire to "destroy everything beautiful I'd never have," akin to the urge to "kill all the fish I couldn't afford to eat, and smother the French beaches I'd never see" (123). In other words, Jack's rage is motivated by a class envy that has turned nihilistic, a sense that if he has been deprived of the world's bounty of beautiful things, then he will destroy all of these so that no one gets to enjoy them.

In its ideal state, Project Mayhem provided a form of playful, implicit protest against patriarchal capitalism. The pranks pulled by its members, such as painting a demon mask on the face of a skyscraper, allowed "sons" to join together in symbolic protest against the economic inequities perpetrated by their bosses and "fathers," the "demons" that built mountains of wealth and then lorded it over others, refusing to share it. But when the sons turn from helping each other become men to taking revenge against the fathers, when the sons turn from trying to build a more equitable world among themselves to destroying their fathers' world and everything in it, including themselves, then Project Mayhem loses its idealism and degenerates into vengeful rage and (self-) destructive nihilism. It is one thing for sons who feel emasculated to empower themselves through fistfights; it is another thing for them to literally castrate their "fathers," as several of the Project Mayhem members do to male authority figures. Similarly, it is one thing for sons to argue for a more equitable distribution of wealth by defacing skyscrapers as symbols of their fathers' power, but it is quite a different thing for sons to plot the literal downfall of these buildings via dynamite, as Tyler orders them to do.

Tyler's message to his boss—"Don't think of this as extinction. Think of this as downsizing" (124)—repeats the same euphemistic excuse his boss gave for firing him, but ups the ante: Tyler is going to "downsize" the entire patriarchal power structure, that is, the whole world, and he is going to do it for revenge. Rather than creating a better world, Tyler's focus is on getting back at the authority figures—fathers, bosses, God—who deprived him of so much of this one; he is enraged at their lack of love for him. On one level, Tyler's violence can be understood as an attempt to provoke the patriarchy into caring enough about him to stop him: "getting God's attention for being bad was better than getting no attention at all. . . . Only if we're caught and punished can we be saved" (141). But on a deeper level, Tyler is so despairing of God's love that, like Satan, he becomes a nihilistic figure, a kind of anti-God dedicated to the destruction of everything. Two of Tyler's proverbs—"You will not be saved" (143) and "Believe in me and you shall die, forever" (145)—indicate that he lacks faith and that he is only leading his followers to extinction.

It is one thing to lose faith in the dubious religion of patriarchal capitalism—that the perfect job or the perfect condo will bring salvation—and replace this faith with a truer one that offers real spiritual fulfillment. But Tyler is too enraged at capitalism's broken promise, too despairing at the failure of that first kind of faith, to really see beyond it to another one. And so, rather than founding a truer faith, he becomes more of a Satanic figure who is bound in vengeful opposition to a capitalistic God. As Palahniuk warns, "Personal power cannot be defined by the 'other' without losing power to that other and becoming used by—a reaction to—that other. Patriarchal or matriarchal or whatever."[32] In his view, "It's time people stopped protesting—and thereby giving more power to their enemy, by reinforcing the enemy with opposition—and humans began to offer their own vision for a better way to live."[33]

Thus Tyler's aggressive masculinity, though it seemed like a solution for Jack, proves in the end to be part of the problem. Conversely, the feminine empathy of another character, Marla, initially appears as a threat, but ultimately Jack finds that it is the answer he seeks. We have already seen how Jack views himself as one of "a generation of men raised by women" (50), so it should not be surprising if at first he wonders whether "another woman is really the answer I need" (51). Being around Marla only makes Jack feel more emasculated. Her dark sarcasm and her suicide attempts seem like a passive surrender to death—precisely the kind of weak, "womanly" response to adversity that he fears in himself.

Marla *is* tempted by self-destructive despair, but she is more honest about her terror of mortality, and more courageous about facing it, than Jack. It is Marla who reaches out to Jack and asks him to feel her breasts for possible lumps, thereby prompting him to recall the time when he feared that he himself might have cancer. And, even though they have both been feigning illness in order to hug and cry at support groups, it is Marla who exposes Jack's fakery, revealing to the terminally ill members that he does not have cancer. Jack's "unmasking and humiliation . . . in front of the support groups he's deceived"[34] is painful but necessary to his growth as a character. He may have been able to cry and sleep as a result of the group meetings, but because he has been lying to the others, Jack has not achieved genuine catharsis, which would require sharing his real fears and weaknesses with them. Jack's lying has been part of a "scam that makes people 'like' [him] without the risk of the character having to be emotionally vulnerable."[35] "The lie gives the narrator power over others. The truth places the narrator at the mercy of others. What's important is how the narrator is brought back to an honest relationship with his community," Palahniuk explained.[36] When Marla exposes Jake's fakery, she brings him one step closer to confessing his real fears, which could enable him to find true solace with the group.

One reason that Jack invents his alternate identity, his Tyler persona, is to give himself the courage to approach Marla, which shows that deep down he knows that he is meant to be with her. Still, even while having sex with her as Tyler, Jack finds a way to keep an *emotional* distance from her, only gradually coming to realize that she is not a threat to him. When Tyler sees that Marla owns a dildo, she quickly tries to reassure him of the adequacy of his manhood. Indeed, since Tyler *is* Jack, he most certainly does have such doubts about his masculinity. As if to prove how virile he is, Tyler has pounding intercourse with Marla all night long. Even though there is a sense in which the sex saves her life by keeping her awake after she took a potentially lethal overdose of pills, Tyler's physical brutality and his abusive language ("Take it, human butt wipe" [64]) seem designed to display his aggressive dominance over her. Such demeaning treatment is only likely to make her feel even more worthless and suicidal. She already has a tendency to refer to herself as "infectious human waste" (61). The next morning, "Marla said she wanted to have Tyler's abortion" (59)—a comment which Tyler admires because it appeals to his nihilistic side. What he callously refuses to see is that her sarcastic remark, a twisted version of "I want to have your baby," is in fact a statement of romantic longing, just as her phone call after taking the pills—"She was doing the big death thing, Marla told me. I should get a move on if I wanted to watch" (59)—was really a cry for help, expressing her wish to be saved.

Marla's underlying desire for romance also comes through in the comment she makes comparing some shoes that Jack is putting on her feet to the condoms discarded by Tyler after sex with her: "the condom is the glass slipper of our generation. You slip it on when you meet a stranger. You dance all night, then you throw it away. The condom, I mean. Not the stranger" (66). In Marla's fractured fairytale, Cinderella seems indifferent to her Prince, just throwing him away, but anyone with a heart can see that she rejects him out of fear that he will reject her. Deep down, her hope is that he will stay. But Tyler is no Prince. When he splices pornographic images of male and female sex organs into family movies where "Cinderella danced with her Prince Charming" (31), Tyler is reducing romance to sex, brutally depriving it of all intimacy and lasting connection. No wonder that, after her time in bed with him, Marla compares herself to one of those Christmas trees dumped on the side of the road like "roadkill animals or sex crime victims" (67). There is nothing joyful or sacred about their relationship. Violent Tyler essentially treats Marla as prey, victimizing her so that he can think himself invulnerable. Such an aggressive persona may have emboldened Jack to approach Marla, but it also ruins any chance of his having a real relationship with her.

In the end, Jack makes some progress toward discovering who he is by having imagined himself as what he is not: Tyler. When Jack finds out that his boss has been blown up—and another man shot—by Tyler, he begins to accept responsibility for his alter ego's actions, finally starting to recognize that he himself committed these destructive deeds. At first, Jack is tempted to take the easy way out, letting others punish him when he provokes a near-suicidal beating from the men at fight club. But when Tyler threatens Marla's life, Jack realizes that there is a significant difference between himself and his alter ego: unlike Tyler, Jack has empathy. He really loves Marla and realizes that he must confront Tyler in order to save her. But at this point Jack does not know that Marla loves him; after all, in his Tyler persona, he has brutally mistreated her. It would seem that, in Marla's eyes, there is no real difference between Jack and Tyler, and Jack himself, overwhelmed by guilt over the misdeeds he perpetrated as Tyler, struggles to see any difference between them. So he decides to save Marla by committing homicide/suicide, to shoot Tyler and therefore also himself, while simultaneously blowing up the building they are standing in—an act of nihilism typical of Tyler. In a sense, Jack has realized he is Tyler but is overidentifying with him, thinking that the only way he can eliminate his enemy is by killing himself because there is essentially no difference between them.

Enter Marla, along with members of the support group, to rescue him. The willingness of these terminally ill persons to risk the remainder of their lives to save him, even after he had initially lied to them, is a moving demonstration of empathy. Moreover, Marla expresses an emotional commitment to him, making it clear that she means Jack, not Tyler, which helps him to realize that there *is* a difference between them. Despite the terrible things Jack did while acting as his alter ego, Marla considers him to be worthy of forgiveness and love. And it is because of this saving difference that, when Jack shoots Tyler and himself, Tyler dies but Jack lives on, for Marla's empathy has made him realize that he can separate from, and be a better person than, his alter ego. Another sign of this separation is that the bomb does not go off; the Jack part of Tyler, secretly hoping to be worthy of Marla's love and therefore of survival, had put the wrong chemical into the explosive mix, thereby saving them all from destruction.

Another way to talk about the separation that Jack makes would be to say that he is neither his former self—empathetic but passive—nor his Tyler persona—assertive but domineering. Instead, what he is becoming is new—someone who combines power with compassion, who feels sympathy for others and is aggressive *in their defense*. The old Jack was too compliant and fearful to fight inequity, and Tyler reacted to injustice by wanting to raze everything to the ground, but the new Jack fights to preserve the best of the past, realizing that it is necessary in order to build a future. Palahniuk has described the old Jack as a "little kid, trying to follow every rule he'd ever been taught," while Tyler is like a teenager in his "rebellious reaction to every rule."[37] Each of these personalities is immature; to develop as a character, Jack must "rise above the either/or choice" and "become an adult, not rebelling against or caving into your culture, but creating a vision of your own and working to make that option into something real."[38] At the end of *Fight Club,* "the personalities are fused back together" when the new Jack "synthesizes both the obedient child and the rebel, and creates a mature human being."[39]

I would argue that Palahniuk here gives an overly optimistic description of Jack's character at the end of the book. Though he may want to move toward synthesis, the Jack we see in the book's final pages still shows signs of schizophrenia. After shooting Tyler and himself, Jack is confined to a mental hospital where another father-figure tries to get him to be a follower and obey society's rules: "a psychiatrist [is] still trying to tell him how he should feel and think."[40] When the psychiatrist tries to get him to ignore social inequities and repeat the platitude that everyone is "special," Jack is tempted to give Tyler's knee-jerk, rebellious reply that everyone is really being treated like "crap," but instead he shows his newfound maturity by avoiding either extreme: "We are not special. We are not crap or trash, either. We just are" (207). Rather than letting himself be defined as some essence, Jack holds open the existentialist possibility that he can make his own meaning in the world, perhaps in loving collaboration with Marla, whom he thinks about phoning from the hospital. But he is not well enough to call her yet. The fact is that Jack still hears voices, the real or imagined whispers of hospital orderlies who claim to be Project Mayhem members waiting for him to return as Tyler and lead their plot to blow up the world. Jack's personality still threatens to split. If he leaves the hospital, he is afraid that his aggressive side will dominate over empathy, that he will become Tyler again and harm Marla. The novel ends with Jack in a state of uncertainty between fusion and fracture, wanting to synthesize his two personalities but paralyzed with fear of their splitting again.

The book's ending is different from that of the film. In the *Fight Club* movie, Marla does not arrive with the support group members to save Jack. Instead, she is brought in by Project Mayhem members, who have seized her upon Tyler's orders, until Jack directs them to let her go. Thus the movie downplays the power of feminine empathy, replacing it with a more conventional scene in which the man takes charge and rescues the woman. Jack does shoot Tyler—and himself—in both versions, enabling Jack to be with Marla, but the movie then introduces an incoherence that is not found in the book. On the one hand, the movie gives added emphasis to the couple's romantic pairing by having Jack and Marla hold hands in the end. This is much more optimistic than the book's conclusion, wherein Jack is still so afraid of his Tyler side that he cannot even phone Marla from the hospital. On the other hand, the movie has some of the bombs that Tyler planted actually detonate, leading to the fall of several surrounding buildings—collapses all the more horrifying in light of the 9/11 terrorist attack on the Twin Towers. Does the film signify the triumph of the couple's love or of Tyler's aggression? Strangely, it seems to signify both at the same time.

Perhaps the most interesting way to read the film's ending is to see it as an exacerbation of the novel's uncertainty. Jack wants romance with Marla but fears that at any moment his destructive Tyler side could come back to menace their love. This threatened resurgence of Tyler is epitomized by the subliminal shot of a penis from a porn film that is spliced into the closing scene of the couple, representing the unconscious aggression that could take control of Jack again. The film thus leaves Jack in an even more indeterminate state than the book, holding hands with his beloved while watching buildings fall—suspended between hope and nihilism, romance and rubble.

Invisible Monsters

Although she may not be schizophrenic like Jack, Shannon McFarland, the narrator of *Invisible Monsters,* is also suffering from an identity crisis. Jack has his white-collar job and his condo; Shannon has her career as a supermodel. Both appear to be successful, but neither has found genuine fulfillment because they feel cut off from any kind of true contact with others: "My first four books take individuals who are isolated in a way that society says should make us happy—isolated by their beauty or career or lovely home—and the plots reintroduce those people back to humanity," Palahniuk has said.[41] We have seen how, for Jack, "Maybe self-destruction is the answer" (49)—letting his perfectly groomed face get pummeled at fight club, blowing up his condo and his office—though in the end he realizes that such violence can go too far and become part of the problem. Shannon, too, chooses self-destruction, taking a shotgun to the lower half of her face in an attempt to escape the beauty trap, the extent to which her identity is based solely on audience approval of her good looks.

And, just as Jack's dilemma was rooted in the author's own life ("I'm the guy who had the Ikea catalogue in my drawer at work," Palahniuk admitted),[42] so Shannon's struggle is related to an identity crisis that Palahniuk found himself facing as he grew older: "My 20s were great, but by the time I was 31, I started to see that I wasn't going to be a young anything much longer, and I was not going to be able to have that sort of energy, that power to walk into a room and be noticed," he said. "I realized that I was gonna have to . . . develop something other than social skills and partygoing skills. . . . So, her face is shot off in an instant, but metaphorically that is the threat of growing older. . . . I was 31 and thought, 'Damn, I have to do something with my life.'"[43] Palahniuk has called *Invisible Monsters* "a 'reverse Cinderella story' where a character gains power by losing her looks."[44] Whereas the traditional version of this fairytale has its heroine gain the Prince's attention when she moves from being covered in ashes to wearing a beautiful ball gown, Palahniuk's rewrite suggests that those with true strength are not dependent on society's superficial judgments of their physical attractiveness or fine attire: "Youth and beauty are power, but not the strongest kind. That's why we must keep growing and finding new forms of power."[45]

But it is not immediately clear whether Shannon's facial disfigurement will be empowering. As an invisible monster, someone with a face so ugly that people cannot bear to look at her, she is able to steal a turkey from a supermarket without anyone stopping her, but what kind of triumph is that? Furthermore, while Shannon may have escaped the positive stereotyping of being seen as a beautiful fashion model, she now risks being pigeonholed as a freak in the eyes of society. After her theft of the turkey, she imagines tabloid headlines that read, "*Monster Girl Steals Festive Holiday Bird*."[46] As Fiorenzo Iuliano has noted, "The monster threatens the paradigms of legitimacy from which it is excluded, but, at the same time, validates and confirms them."[47] Shannon's mutilated face may seem like an affront to society, but as long as people consider that face to be "ugly," then the definition of what is "beautiful" goes unchallenged; the norms of beauty remain in place. Having escaped the beauty trap, Shannon risks being imprisoned in "ugliness," which is just another form of the same trap. As another character warns her, "if you can find any way out of our culture, then that's a trap, too. Just wanting to get out of the trap reinforces the trap" (220).

Shannon also has to contend with the consequences of her disfigurement. Her fiancé, Manus Kelley, loses interest in her and is instead attracted to her fashion model friend, Evie Cottrell, and to another gorgeous woman, Brandy Alexander. Shannon's face may have changed, but her mind is still thinking in the same old ways, drawing her sense of self-worth from a man, wanting to best her rivals for his attention. Thus, even though Shannon's physical appearance has been drastically altered, she still imagines herself modeling for a fashion photographer, striking poses to win his—and everyone's—approval. To win back Manus, Shannon considers getting reconstructive surgery to restore what she had before the shotgun blast took off her lower jaw, rendering her mutilated and mute: "The photographer in my head says: Give me a voice. Flash. Give me a face" (112). Note that Shannon is not so much expressing what she wants as she is parroting what she thinks she's supposed to want. Society expects her to look good and speak seductively in order to attract a man. "Hearing the voice of the photographer in her own head," Shannon "internalizes the policing mechanism of those in power," as Scott Ash puts it,[48] using language from philosopher Michel Foucault. Palahniuk was inspired by a number of Foucault's ideas, particularly the notion that society's norms are enforced not only by actual police but also by our own internalization of these norms, like the beauty trap, which makes it difficult even to imagine a way out of them. Prisons can be psychological, too.

Initially, the photographer's commands in Shannon's head show her repeating verbatim what society dictates she should want, as in "Give me youth and energy and innocence and beauty. Flash" (176). When Manus averts his gaze from her damaged face, her thoughts reveal her continued dependency on him: "Give me pity. Flash. Give me another chance" (41). Even when it turns out that her fiancé may like men more than women or that he may love himself more than anyone else, she still clings to the idea of a model marriage, to what society says he and she should have: "Give me romance. Flash. Give me denial" (69) of the truth about him. The fact, though, that Shannon admits she is in "denial" shows that she is no longer merely parroting society's demands but beginning to recognize that real people often diverge from them.

Manus may not be the only one whose desire for adulation, whose need to *receive* love, makes it difficult to *offer* love to others; Shannon herself has this problem. She remembers the time when her brother Shane, with whom she had always competed for attention, came to her window for help and she refused him, turning off the light in her room so that only her own face remained reflected in the glass. "Give me denial" and "Give me ignorance," she thinks (150), now that she sees how stupid and cruel she was to have put herself first and not to have recognized *his* need for her love. When jealous Shannon burns Evie's clothes, her first thoughts are "Give me total and complete justified retribution" (158), but already there seems to be some irony in the overemphasis, as if Shannon is unsuccessfully defending herself against her own conscience, half-realizing that she is putting on a jealous act because that is what women who are rivals in love are expected to do. Back when she and Evie were still friends, they used to put on mock performances of formulaic female fury: "we'd wear high heels and pretend to slap each other across the mouth because of some guy we both wanted" (72).

Planning to wreak vengeance on both her female rivals by having Evie shoot Brandy, Shannon thinks, "Give me violent revenge fantasies as a coping mechanism. Flash" (181). A space for irony has opened up between Shannon and the photographer's voice in her head; she is no longer just repeating the social script but *aware* that she is repeating it "as a coping mechanism." Even as she plans to follow this script and get the better of her rivals, she is conscious of herself as performing a role for the public, "plotting my big revenge in the spotlight" (181). What Shannon has loathed in the other two women—their insatiable need to be the center of attention—is now something that she is beginning to recognize in herself. When she sets a fire—to be blamed on Brandy—that burns Evie's wedding dress and her hair, Shannon is tempted to think that "even the biggest tragic fire, it's just a sustained chemical reaction. The oxidation of Joan of Arc" (15). However, Shannon realizes that this blasé attitude, this scientific distance, is not what she really feels. "Give me detached existentialist ennui" and "Give me rampant intellectualism as a coping mechanism," she thinks (13), both feeling detached *and* recognizing that this is a coping mechanism for truer, deeper feelings that she is struggling to deal with.

When Evie shoots Brandy, who lies there apparently dying, Shannon attempts to move beyond the scripted emotions of retributive rage and summon her real feelings, but she is so addicted to performing that she struggles to express anything that is not prefabricated to please an audience: "unless the meter is running and some photographer is yelling: Give me empathy" and there is the "flash" of a camera (17), Shannon is at a loss for emotion. And yet ironically it is through realizing just how addicted to attention they all are, how similar she is to Brandy and Evie in this regard, that Shannon is able to express her true fellow feeling for them, and most especially her empathy for Brandy. "Even when I'm not getting paid [as a photographer's model], I can give love and happiness and charm," she realizes in the end (295)—and importantly there is no "flash" this time because she is no longer acting for an audience; her feeling for others comes from herself.

If Shannon is able to get in touch with herself, to find some sense of personal identity, it is mostly through her relationship with Brandy. Yet Brandy, who is a male-to-female transsexual undergoing operations to make her look like a gorgeous fashion model, would seem to be the epitome of the beauty trap that Shannon was trying to escape when she shot herself in the face: artificial and obsessed with appearance because always starved for attention. Shannon's love/hate relationship with Brandy is something that readers have tended to find puzzling. Sonia Baelo-Allué notes that, "paradoxically, the narrator rejects her past as a fashion model for everything it represents but she is willing to participate in the shallow world of Brandy,"[49] and according to Richard Viskovic and Eluned Summers-Bremer, Shannon "frequently reiterates her disgust for the large show that is Brandy Alexander, while following in her footsteps like a helpless thrall."[50] It is true that Brandy represents the temptation for Shannon to fall back into the superficial world of looks and adulation. Not only does Brandy suggest that Shannon have reconstructive surgery to restore her beautiful face, but Brandy has directed her own surgeons to make herself look exactly the way Shannon did before the disfigurement. Brandy thus personifies the lure of narcissism, professional—fashion modeling—and personal; she is the mirror of Shannon's former self. Shannon realizes: "What I love is myself. I was so beautiful" (198).

Brandy takes Shannon and Manus on a road trip across the Pacific Northwest where, donning various kinds of clothing as disguises and assuming a variety of fake names, they con their way into wealthy homes, pretending to be potential buyers, in order to steal prescription drugs, which they then sell to support themselves. For Shannon, this con involving false identities reflects on the other con that is Brandy's "false" identity, making it seem as though her passing herself off as a beautiful woman is similarly shameful, a comparable sham. When Shannon thinks of Brandy's elaborate hairdo as "some strawberry auburn mushroom cloud rising over a Pacific atoll" (27), this comparison to a "bombshell" conveys both an attraction to the power of Brandy's beauty and a fear of its devastation, for that beauty is also loathed as something artificial and hollow. As Brandy leads Shannon to keep changing her own hair, clothing, and name while they rob house after house, Shannon fears that she is being seduced into her friend's world of artificiality and pretense: "I hate it when Brandy changes our lives without warning. Sometimes, twice in one day, you have to live up to a new identity." When Shannon then compares the anxiety of these changes to the "stress the constantly mutating AIDS virus must feel" (64), it is clear that she fears being turned into a carrier of Brandy's disease, of herself becoming artificial and identity-less, all appearance and no substance. Since Brandy looks the way Shannon used to and keeps encouraging her to change her appearance in the ways that she once did as a fashion model, Shannon feels that she is being drawn back into that realm of sham selves, as in the scene where the two women are seated in the mirrored bathroom of a wealthy home and Shannon sees "just too many Brandy Alexanders to count, and they're all being the boss of me" (28).

But Brandy is more than just a negative example of the appearance-obsessed, fashion-model world that is better left behind, and Shannon's attraction to her is more than just the temptation of returning to that realm. Brandy is also a positive role model for Shannon, in ways that only gradually become clear to her. When Brandy introduces herself, she points sequentially to her prodigious breasts, the pearls around her neck, her towering hair, and her luscious lips, saying "This . . . is the Princess Brandy Alexander" (25). At first,

Shannon may tend to see in this a pathetic admission that Brandy is nothing but her artificial parts—implants, accessories, coiffure, collagen—but in Brandy's case the whole is greater than the sum of the parts. Rather than believing that these parts are her identity, Brandy is *aware* of their artificiality. Rather than let herself be used by the fashion industry, by a society that dictates how women should look, Brandy *takes control* of the fashion codes and uses them to *express herself.* Brandy deploys an ever-changing array of feminine signifiers to create the image of herself that she wants to project at any given time. Instead of being caught in the beauty trap, Brandy escapes it by consciously performing femininity in a grand manner that enacts the gender stereotypes but does so in her own inimitable way.

At the same time, she remains aware that "Brandy Alexander" both is and is not herself. It is a sham through which she expresses some real truths. For example, when Brandy winks at Shannon, this could be seen as a cute cliché, a pretended connection that is just Brandy acting the part of "the understanding woman," but that is not the way the wink is intended or received: "God should be able to wink that good," thinks Shannon. "Like somebody taking your picture. Give me joy. Give me fun. Give me love. Flash" (47). Shannon wants true recognition beyond the superficial kind given to her by the photographer's camera, and she is beginning to sense that Brandy's interest in her might be genuine; her understanding and her love could be real. When a speech therapist fails to understand what Shannon really needs, Brandy comments that such people "can be *so* stupid about these situations" (60). Brandy's emphasis on "*so*," the adverb, rather than "stupid," the adjective, is part of her feminine speech performance, but at the same time she really means what she says, understanding and empathizing with Shannon more than the therapist does.

When Brandy points to the artificial parts—breasts, pearls, hair, lips—that are her hyper-feminine image, she uses her "enormous" male hands—"the one part about Brandy Alexander the surgeons couldn't change," so she "doesn't even try and hide" them (23). Neither masculine nor feminine in the conventional sense, Brandy transcends gender stereotypes by mixing and matching them: "Just by herself," she creates her own "shift in the beauty standard" (58). Rather than losing herself in conformity to society's norms, Brandy plays with those conventions to make herself into what she wants to be. As neither her male hands nor her otherwise feminine appurtenances, the real Brandy is the spirit inhabiting these, the will behind her ever-changing outward appearance.

This will to change is rooted in Brandy's preoperative past, when she was a teenage boy named Shane—in fact, Shannon's brother. Lionized as a high-school sports hero, Shane nevertheless felt trapped in that gender stereotype, much as Shannon, despite being a successful supermodel, felt caught in the beauty trap. Like Shannon, who shot herself in the face to escape, Shane disfigured himself with an exploding can of hairspray so that he would no longer be everyone's golden boy. However, when a policeman investigating the "accident" abused him, leaving him with a venereal disease, his parents assumed that Shane was gay and forced him to leave home. Having gone from "basketball king" to "King of Fag Town" (96), Shane was trapped again in another stereotype, this time a negative one, much as Shannon came to be seen as a "monster." Shane opts for transsexual surgery not because he feels his real sex is female, and he cross-dresses and gives a queenly performance not because he believes he is really feminine, but in order to escape all sex/gender stereotyping. "What is it going to take to break out and establish some modicum of freedom, despite all the cultural training that's been our entire existence?" asks Palahniuk. He explains that Shane "doesn't really want a sex change" but that "having it was the most important thing [he] could think to do, because it would destroy an identity that was being imposed upon [him] by society."[51]

And so the various names Shane/Brandy assumes and the various disguises he/she adopts while on the road trip are not just an impersonation scam to steal drugs; they are playful yet serious attempts to escape society's identity traps and claim the freedom to be oneself in the moment. "I'm not straight, and I'm not gay," Brandy says. "I'm not bisexual. I want out of the labels" (261). Male or female, masculine or feminine, straight or gay—even intersex, androgynous, or bisexual—all become ways of pigeonholing people, and Brandy, by choosing to enact and embody different parts of these categories at different times, rejects being labeled as any one of them. In this, Brandy is like Palahniuk himself, who stated that "I know people who have spun their nationality or their sexuality or their race, but after a few books it's really limiting and their readership doesn't want them to write about anything other than that experience. . . . They find themselves pigeonholed, documenting the same small aspect of self over and over";[52] "God forbid I get moved to that ghetto called the 'Gay and Lesbian Shelf.'"[53]

Brandy's claiming the right to invent and reinvent her own identity has implications for the special kind of road trip she takes. Just as Brandy is transsexual more in the sense of being between sexes than in definitively changing from male to female, so her road trip has no clear destination, neither the conventional one dictated by society—male and masculine—nor its simple opposite—female and feminine. Rather, as Brandy puts it, "I want to find something else, unknowable, some place to be that's not on the map. A real adventure"—"Not just a story that goes and then, and then, and then, and then until you die" (261). In sympathy with Brandy's aspirations, Palahniuk's novel was not written as a straightforward story but as a work that jumps here and there, changing character names and scene settings in an unorthodox fashion to the point where the reader may feel as Shannon does: "It's hard to remember who I started this road trip being" (64). As the author has explained, "We're taking a road trip, but it's not towards a specific ending. I think that quality of directed randomness or searching randomness is echoed by the structure of the book—that aggressive searching without a pre-conceived idea of what the end is going to be."[54] "Directed randomness" is a seeming contradiction in terms, yet it captures that sense of a search for personal identity that is at the same time a refusal to settle for any one of society's prescribed categories, its expected destinations or destinies.

In its very first form—an early version of the novel that has now been published, with some newly added elements, as *Invisible Monsters Remix*—the book was even more "searchingly random," with lines directing readers to jump back and forth between earlier and later chapters, and with some sections of the book as entirely separate side roads or byways that can only be found by departing from the novel's already twisty main route. Contrasting his work with a linear novel whose characters are defined when they reach a clear destination, Palahniuk has compared his book to a shopping catalog or a fashion magazine with articles that jump unexpectedly to some other page or with ads that appear on unnumbered pages, in uncharted territory. The reader's "road trip" through the book would thus be a journey of surprise and discovery rather than a pre-charted path. As the author explained, "Even after the reader reached the words 'The End' she'd still sense she hadn't read it all. The book would still hold some lingering secrets. You could open it again and find something—as with the Sears catalogue or *Vogue* magazine or anyone you love—something that you'd never seen before";[55] "you'll realize that this chaotic, beautiful thing is ultimately unknowable, like a person"[56]—like Brandy Alexander.

In the end, Brandy completes her sex reassignment surgery so that she looks just like Shannon, who gives Brandy all her identification papers and her modeling career. But was not the whole point of Brandy Alexander that her story had no set ending, that she kept reinventing herself so as not to be trapped in one identity, and most especially not in the stereotypical role of fashion model? The end of *Invisible Monsters* has been the cause of some consternation for critics. Shannon's "act of bequeathing her identity and career to Shane/Brandy is a highly ambiguous gesture, given that [Shannon] took such drastic and painful measures to escape that identity and career herself," argues Sherry R. Truffin,[57] and Sonia Baelo-Allué sees Brandy as giving up her ever-changing or "liquid" existence for a fixed identity that is all about appearance and social approval: "The character that has most passionately defended liquid life finally receives a solid identity she can fit into seamlessly," one that "does not belong to" her and that "turns her new body into the mark of success on which to depend."[58] There does seem to be some danger that Brandy will make the same mistake Shannon did of living a life only for public adulation, of letting her identity be dictated by photographers—both the real ones and those in her head.

But Brandy, though she looks like her sister, is not Shannon. With the ever-present reminder of her male hands, Brandy is *aware* that her passing as Shannon is an impersonation; her fabulous feminine attire is a masquerade. Whereas Shannon felt driven by a need for attention to become what others wanted her to be, Brandy *chooses* the role of supermodel, putting together unique ensembles as a show of self-expression. Rather than merely following fashion dictates, Brandy could escape the beauty trap by redefining the beauty standard as the world's first transsexual supermodel. A leader and not just a follower, a role model for those who want to be themselves rather than for those who conform to fashion trends, Brandy could revolutionize the role of supermodel. As Shannon advises her, "Find value in what we've been taught is worthless. Find good in what the world says is evil" (294). Andy Johnson asks us to "Imagine the controversy if a covertly transgendered person won *America's Next Top Model* or became *Miss America*. Shannon has placed her brother in a position to become such a beauty icon, and the result will allow them to challenge American society's assumptions and fears."[59] Or, as Shannon says, "I wish the whole world would embrace what it hates" (294)—that people would fall in love with the fabulous Brandy and then realize that the beauty they adore is a transsexual.

As for Shannon, she chooses neither to have facial reconstructive surgery so that people will again see her as conventionally beautiful, nor to accept society's view of her disfigurement as monstrously ugly. Instead, she redefines the beauty standard in her own way. First, she examines her facial features as they are now and refuses the labels for them: "They aren't good or bad, ugly or beautiful. They're just the way I look" (296). Then, having discarded the narratives that others have tried to write for her, including Brandy's suggestion that she remake herself back into a supermodel, Shannon plots her own course, not following Brandy's example exactly but being inspired by the other's courage to reinvent herself. "What I need is a new story," Shannon decides. "What Brandy's been doing for me. What I need to learn to do for myself. To write my own story" (296). In *Invisible Monsters Remix,* in one of the "side road" chapters off from the main narrative, Shannon writes her own fairytale ending to her "reverse Cinderella story"[60] where even a girl without the usual "good looks" can meet and marry her Prince Charming, because the "groom is someone discerning. A connoisseur who won't settle for one-size-fits-all beauty. He's someone who can appreciate a cubist face. . . . It's *Pretty Woman* but with a less conventional definition of *pretty*."[61]

Survivor

Where Shannon and Brandy, each in different ways, struggle to create their own identities "based on fashion and fantasy," and where Jack seeks to define himself "based on what [he is] not" (his opposite, Tyler), Tender Branson in *Survivor* works on "creating [himself] in the face of immortality."[62] Tender is one of the remaining survivors of a religious cult, the Creedish, who committed mass suicide rather than be subjected to an FBI investigation. Tender, who has spent some years employed as a domestic in rich people's homes while sending his wages back to fund the church compound, is expected to prove his faith by following the others and committing suicide, thereby achieving "deliverance," but he has begun to doubt whether killing himself is really the way to immortality. He has had enough exposure to the outside world to doubt his elders' creed, but he has not yet found or invented a faith of his own to give meaning to his existence.

One of the first steps on Tender's tortuous path to self-discovery is when he answers calls to a suicide hotline, only to tell people to kill themselves. In a sense, he becomes the mouthpiece for his religious creed, dictating that others do what church doctrine has said all the faithful should do. Yet Tender does not follow his own advice, and he has moved beyond an unquestioning adherence to the Creedish faith. He is well aware that, when desperate people call the crisis intervention line, they do not expect to be told to commit suicide. Thus, when he refers to himself as a "Messiah" or "Savior" or "Part-time god,"[63] he is quite conscious of the irony: he knows that the callers do not believe that the suicide he advises will mean "deliverance"—and neither, anymore, does he. Tender realizes that he is playing God, arrogating to himself a kind of power that may feel good to him—"It's a rush, having that kind of control"—but that destroys others and is bad for his soul, for what he is committing amounts to "murder" (280). Tender tells himself that "People don't want their lives fixed" because then "what would they have left? Just the big scary unknown" (282). However, he is the one who avoids solving his own problems out of fear that, if he succeeded, he would then have to face the resulting freedom, the need to decide for himself what to do with his life. Tender tells himself that "this is a terrible world" and that, in counseling a caller to commit suicide, he "ended his suffering" (280), yet once again Tender is projecting onto others: it is the mass suicide of the cult—his only family—that has made him see the world as a terrible place. Similarly, Tender's argument that callers might as well kill themselves because "everything you love will die" (277) is rooted more in his fatalistic response to his own particular circumstances than in any understanding of the callers' lives.

Palahniuk suggests that the underlying reason why Tender begins answering the crisis hotline is "in order to meet people as damaged as himself."[64] Despite his murderous advice, deep down Tender wants a support group to give him help so that he can heal and live. Thus, when he pretends to be more interested in breading a veal cutlet than in listening to sufferers' woes, when he lets desperate callers hear him flushing the toilet so that they will know he "couldn't care less" (278), his indifference is really an act to cover up his caring too much. If he lets himself feel for these people and cannot save them, the way he could not save the members of his family in the cult, then he fears that his own suffering will be unbearable, a prolongation of his grief over the mass suicide. When a caller named Trevor tells about having prophetic dreams of people he cannot save from dying in plane crashes, Tender knows why Trevor is suicidal, for he feels the same way about his own inability to prevent the mass suicide. In an attempt to kill this feeling in himself, Tender advises Trevor to commit suicide, which he does. Later, Tender tries to convince himself that Trevor's death was "nothing that really mattered" (280), but this feigned apathy is belied by Tender's fervent hope that Trevor, along with all the other callers who have killed themselves, will rise from the grave in pursuit of their murderous messiah: "I want to be chased by flesh-eating zombies" (255). If these sufferers were to take revenge on Tender for his killing counsel, not only could he believe that there was some moral order to the universe, but he would also have "proof that death isn't the end" (255). Tender would rather be killed by vengeful ghouls than continue to live in a world without feeling or faith.

Tender's next step on his wayward journey to self-discovery occurs when, standing at Trevor's tomb and pretending to have been his friend, he meets the man's sister, Fertility. Because Tender is not yet ready to acknowledge his own guilt over the part he played in her brother's suicide, he hides this truth about himself from Fertility. It turns out that she, like her brother, has been having dreams of future disasters. Increasing despair over her inability to prevent disasters then leads her to call the crisis hotline, where Tender, speaking anonymously and not revealing that he is the one she met at the mausoleum, advises her *not* to commit suicide but instead to date her brother's "friend"—that is, himself. On one level, the advice is self-serving: Tender pretends to be a grief counselor helping her out, when in fact he is helping himself by taking advantage of her distress. But on another level, Tender's selfish, conniving advice is an attempt to make a true connection that could be beneficial to them both. When Tender tells her that this is "a perfect chance to bring love and supportive nurturing support to a man who needs your love desperately" (234), the verbal redundancy shows that he is mouthing clichés, but hidden inside this rhetorical sham is a genuine truth about the real needs of Tender himself. Similarly, when Tender advises her to "Let your mutual loss bring the two of you together" (235), he is lying about having been Trevor's close friend, but Tender does feel depressed and guilty over her brother's death, and he too has lost members of his own family in the mass suicide, much as Fertility lost her brother along with all the others whom she could not save from the disasters she foresaw.

The very fact that Tender reaches out to a woman, even in a guarded way, is remarkable, given that the church elders trained him to avoid sex. When he was a child, they made him watch women suffering the pangs of childbirth and sometimes dying in labor, while the elders preached that "the wages of sex was death" (34). Now, when Fertility tries to get him to talk dirty to her on the phone, Tender hears reproving Bible verses in his head, telling him to "Flee fornication" (237) and warning him of how Eve tempted Adam, causing mankind's fall into sin: "she gave me of the tree, and I did eat" (234), "For some are already turned aside after Satan" (233). Matters are not made any better when, in addition to Fertility's phone-sex voice—"Tell me what you want me to do. Make me do something terrible" (201)—Tender also finds out about the "terrible [job] she does to earn money" (206): Fertility hires herself out as a surrogate mother but knows she is barren and so cannot conceive. Her paid sex with other women's husbands thus amounts to fraud, adultery, and prostitution. When Fertility yells out a "porn goddess orgasm scream" to him on the phone (233), Tender fears that all her interest in him is merely a sham, that he is just another one of her johns, another occasion for sin.

What Tender gradually comes to understand is that Fertility does not want to bring a child into this world for she sees it as a place "pregnant" with unpreventable disasters. Her prophecies of doom have made her leery of love and conception, much as Tender's cult training has affected him. Yet both of them desire to make a true human connection and to overcome their despair over the future of humanity. Tender's increased understanding of Fertility occurs in what may seem to be an unlikely location: a men's restroom. Peering through a hole between his toilet stall and the one next to him, Tender can see Fertility's red lips and wet tongue telling him about future disasters: "I listened at the hole the way I listened to people confess over the telephone, the way I listened at crypts for signs of life" (110). Fertility's porn-goddess act on the phone was nevertheless a real attempt to connect with Tender, just as the "glory holes" in the stalls (113), ostensibly made to facilitate sexual contact between their occupants, could represent a desire for a more meaningful relationship, a truer glory. See also the graffiti on the walls, which is both crudely sexual ("I suck and swallow") and romantically hopeful ("I only want to love her if she'd just give me the chance" [112]). Fertility's porn-goddess lips want love, just as her despairing voice on the suicide hotline wanted a reason to live. She tells Tender about the disasters she's foreseen in the hope that he can somehow alter the future and save lives, including his and her own. If Tender had wanted zombies to rise from their crypts as a way of changing the past—the suicidal cult and Trevor would no longer be dead—Fertility wants Tender to prove to her that the future is not an entirely foregone conclusion, that there is still some hope of fulfillment in this life, some joyful surprises before the end.

Unfortunately, Tender's growing connection to Fertility has reawakened his fear of the pain he would feel were he to lose her, as he has lost so many others. To defend himself against further grief, Tender distances himself from Fertility, attempting to numb all feeling and to rise above all perishable flesh. As he now appears to be the sole survivor of the Creedish cult, the public is fascinated with him, and Tender lets a media agent turn him into a celebrity spiritual leader. As part of this process, he submits to a series of drug treatments and surgical enhancements so that he will fit the image of the muscular Christ that is currently in fashion. One result of his steroid use is that his arms become too big for him to tie his own shoes. With this image, Palahniuk shows Tender growing ever more distant from common humanity or any grounding in his own body. As a famous preacher, Tender is worshipped and adored by millions—"loved without the risk of loving anyone in return" (129). Watching his own image on the monitor during the taping of a television show, he imagines leaving his perishable body behind and ascending to a heavenly afterlife: "My whole body feels as far away and detached as the picture of me wearing a black suit and sitting on a brown sofa on the studio monitor, the way it's supposed to feel as your soul goes up to Heaven and watches the rest of you, the flesh and blood of you, die" (105).

Tender's disconnection from the physical realm makes him callous toward humanity, including Fertility. Since he thinks of himself as having transcended the weakness of the flesh, he can self-righteously condemn her for her surrogate-mother scam, calling her an "ADULTEROUS DEVIL WHORE" (101) when she confesses in a phone call to his televangelist show. Yet Palahniuk hints that it is not the true Tender who says these terrible words; rather, he reads them off the teleprompter with his collagen-injected lips: "With no feeling in my lips, I just say what they tell me to say" (101). The implication is that, if Tender were to speak for himself and admit his true feeling for Fertility, he would empathize with her as a mortal sinner like himself and forgive her. Deep down Tender knows that he has not really "evolved beyond physical needs" (104), that becoming famous has not really made him immortal, and that by behaving immorally, by denying his own humanity and mistreating others, he is not saving his body or his soul: “The truth is that all this was just part of the suicide process” (134); “I see myself dead and in Hell” (132).

Fertility helps to get Tender back on the right path when she rescues him just as he is about to appear in a fake wedding ceremony arranged by his media agent as part of a Super Bowl halftime show. Metaphorically, she saves him for a real marriage—to her. Tender’s reentry into physical reality following his televised fantasy also involves eschewing all cosmetic surgeries and body-enhancing drugs. As he feels his tan disappearing, his teeth yellowing, and his muscles sagging, Tender fears that he is dying, but Fertility says she is “saving” his “life” (54), for it is only by admitting his own mortal flaws that he can recognize his common bond with others and forgive them their weaknesses, as he hopes to have his forgiven. Indeed, Tender now apologizes for having called her a whore and confesses the role he played in encouraging her brother to commit suicide, and Fertility forgives him. Rather than dreading sex with her as sinful, Tender attempts to free his mind from Creedish doctrine and give his virginity to Fertility. As another character tells him, “You’ll be a slave the rest of your life unless you bite the apple” (40).

But Palahniuk insists that lifelong fears are not so easily overcome. Tender is still troubled by Fertility’s past of having sex for pay, and while she warns him that she may have picked up a fatal disease, his suicidal tendencies lead him to decline to wear a condom. It would seem that some part of him still associates sex with sin and death. Perhaps this is why, when they do make love, he does not enter her deeply before ejaculating prematurely. Beyond the nervousness of a virgin, there is a despairing sense of her and of himself, a lack of faith that their love could have a future, which keeps him from truly connecting. For her part, Fertility, who thought she was barren, miraculously conceives a child from this encounter, but she still struggles with the thought that it would be cruel to bring a newborn into this world of disasters, the deaths she dreams about yet has been unable to prevent. The superficiality of Tender’s love and his fatalism about the future do not help her.

Fertility tells Tender that she has foreseen another disaster: a man will hijack a plane and crash it into the Australian Outback. Fertility, carrying their unborn child, gets on that plane. Fertility’s act can be seen as a test of the power of Tender’s love and the strength of his belief in their future. At first, he shows some promise of passing that test. Despite his fatalistic tendencies, he rushes to the plane in an effort to identify the hijacker and stop him from crashing it with his beloved on board. Then, when Tender realizes that *he is* the hijacker—he is the only man with a gun—he lands the plane, rescues Fertility and all the passengers by letting them off, and, after he is airborne again, lets the pilot parachute to safety. What Tender has realized is that just because death is inevitable does not mean that life in the meantime has to be meaningless. "Long-term," Fertility has said, "we're all going to die," but "Short-term" there is the possibility that we can "live happily ever after" (50). Tender's realization that he is the hijacker is a metaphor for his recognizing that, by devaluing life due to fear of its end, he has only been making matters worse, hastening the very disaster he wants to fend off. Tender may not be able to control everything in the end, but this does not mean that his actions are without effect in the here and now. By saving Fertility along with the other passengers, he proves his love for her and his belief in the power he has to preserve the near-future.

But it is not clear whether Tender has sufficient faith in himself to overcome the fatalistic influences of his past. The conclusion of *Survivor* is equivocal about whether he passes Fertility's test. On the one hand, it would seem that Tender goes down with the plane, "trapped here, in my nosedive, in my life," with "so many things I want to change but can't" (1). If that is the case, then all we have is his life story as narrated by him into the airplane's flight recorder/black box, a fatalistic story with its inevitable countdown—the pages are numbered in reverse—to death by plane crash. On the other hand, there is evidence that Tender, aided by Fertility's helpful hints which show her faith in him, may have figured out a way to bail out before the crash while still seeming to be talking into the flight recorder as the plane hits the ground. Tender has reason to fake his death in order to elude authorities who want to arrest him for crimes he did not commit.

Fertility predicts that he will indeed find a way to leave his "screwed-up life story"—not his life—"behind," and that after the crash he will be "dead to the whole world" (6), which is not necessarily the same as being dead. Those attending carefully to Tender's tale may also have noted a passing mention of "microcassette recorders" on the plane (8) and of his having to "use the bathroom" (287). According to Palahniuk, it is possible that at a certain point during the flight Tender is "actually in the bathroom dictating the last chapter [of his life story] into the cassette recorder." He takes this with him into the cockpit where, just moments before the crash, "he starts the cassette talking, then bails out, into Fertility's waiting arms. . . . The rest of the book is just one machine whirring and bitching to another machine."[65]

Palahniuk has said that "I had to write the ending open enough that people could either figure it out and get the happy ending, or they could read the unhappy ending"; thus, "people" could "take from it what they wanted."[66] I would argue that, just as Fertility tests Tender, so Palahniuk tests his readers. Those who tend to see the past as a fatal determinant of the future will believe that Tender came to a bad end. Alternatively, those with faith in the power of love to change the future for the better, at least in the short term, will imagine Tender in Fertility's arms rather than death's embrace. Which ending do *you* see?

Choke

Choke, the fourth novel in Palahniuk's identity tetralogy, incorporates elements from the previous three books. As in *Survivor,* where Tender was suicidal over the death of his family, Victor Mancini in *Choke* is depressed and despairing as he gradually loses his mother, Ida, to dementia. In his mother's younger years, she was a social anarchist, pulling anti–status quo stunts like those of Tyler and Project Mayhem in *Fight Club.* Now that Ida is dying in a hospice, Victor seeks comfort by pretending to choke on food and then being saved and cradled by restaurant patrons, much as *Fight Club*'s Jack pretended to have an incurable disease so that he could find solace in the arms of terminally ill patients at therapy groups. Victor also attends therapy groups under false pretenses: he goes to meetings of sex addicts, not because he is seeking recovery but in order to find further bed partners. Although he is tempted by love for one woman, Paige, Victor insists on keeping all his sexual encounters casual so that he can avoid the pain that comes with feeling, much as Jack distanced himself from Marla in *Fight Club* and Tender avoided Fertility in *Survivor.* Feigning total callousness, Victor defies conventional wisdom and adopts as his behavioral motto "*What would Jesus* NOT *do?*"[67] much as Shannon in *Invisible Monsters,* refusing to conform to social expectations for a woman, shot herself in the face and became a "monster." However, Victor eventually swings from despair to grandiose hope and comes to believe that he represents the Second Coming of Christ, supposedly enabling him to save everyone, which recalls how Tender in *Survivor* went from being suicidal to masquerading as the Messiah.

For some readers, the similarities between *Choke* and previous novels make it a derivative and diminished work. According to *Washington Post* critic G. Beato, "Much of the material comes off as a lesser writer's efforts to imitate Palahniuk's obsessions and tone." This reviewer argues that *Choke* "illustrates the downside of creating your own genre: if you stick too closely to your rules and formulas, you begin to sound generic."[68] I hope to show that *Choke* is as nuanced and complex as *Fight Club, Invisible Monsters,* and *Survivor* and thus does not represent a slide into redundancy or self-parody.

Choke's protagonist, Victor, has a lot of problems, and he tends to blame all of them on his mother. We recall that in *Fight Club* Jack and Tyler had suffered from distant and absent fathers. "In a way I felt I bashed fathers so much," Palahniuk has said, "that's why I had to do *Choke* and take a few swings at mothers to even the score."[69] Victor's mother, Ida, is both distant and too close. She is a single mother so there has always been only Ida and Victor, yet she stole him out of a baby stroller; she is neither his biological nor his legal mother. In and out of jails and mental institutions her entire life due to her antisocial acts and experimental drug use, Ida has spent many years apart from Victor, yet each time she is freed, she kidnaps him from his foster mother and the two of them bond as closely as criminals on the run. When Victor, now that he is a young adult, chokes in restaurants so that he can be saved by strangers who in a sense adopt him, cradling him and afterward sending him birthday cards with money, it is because he seeks a surrogate parent, having felt abandoned so many times by Ida, who left him every time she was arrested. "Why you do this is so infantile" (49), Victor's friend Denny says about the choking stunts, and he is more right than he realizes. The choking is even more complicated since we find out that the first time Victor did it was when, as a boy, he deliberately stuffed a corn dog down his throat in order to alert authorities to his presence and prompt them to arrest his mother for kidnapping. Choking is thus imbued with guilt for Victor, a repeated punishing of himself for "betraying" his mother, even as it expresses his desire to be loved by a reliable parent.

During their time together, when Ida would insist that Victor say he loves her and hates his young foster mothers, she sounded more like a jealous spouse than a caring parent. Though she would allege that they had abused him, Ida is the one who could more accurately be accused of child abuse. On one occasion, just before Ida is arrested again, she spray-painted the contours of Victor's shadow on a wall, comparing it to how a "girl traced the outline of her lover's shadow" (4) so that she could remember him after he was gone. Here the far-reaching extent of Ida's "love" for her "son" is undercut by an element of incestuous possessiveness. Ida also made it clear that she expected him to do great things with his life and then return to show "how he's grown into the exact outline she'd planned for him" by tracing his shadow (6). A mother's high hopes for her son can become unrealistic expectations and impossible dreams, which Victor discovers when, after excelling in medical school to fulfill Ida's wish for him to be a "doctor saving people" (5), he then drops out—presumably due to his growing realization that he will not be able to save everyone, but additionally because he needs the tuition money to pay the hospital bills for his mother, whom he also cannot save.

Thus, Ida's idealistic hopes may have been meant as encouragement, but when Victor cannot live up to them, he feels like a failure, causing him to succumb to despair. Similarly, Ida's anarchic acts are designed to free him from a life of social conformity. "I stole you out of a stroller," she says, "to save you from the kind of life you'd get" with an ordinary mother (269), but seeing her get arrested again and again has had the opposite effect, making him extremely risk-averse, "terrified to do anything except what everybody else did. Anything new or different or original was probably against the law" (157). And the most significant risk that Victor is afraid to take is that of loving someone, for his feelings for his mother have been met with repeated abandonment—though Ida would claim that she loves him more than any other mother could and that she left him only when she was forcibly taken away by the authorities.

Victor's sex addiction is a way of being with women without developing the affection for them that would make him vulnerable to feeling their loss. The words that he uses to describe his encounters reveal a great deal about his attitude toward his partners and himself. During a liaison with a woman in an airplane lavatory, Victor sees their reflections in a mirror—"flat and behind glass . . . a magazine picture, somebody else, not us, somebody beautiful with a life or a future outside this moment" (255). Here is sex as escapist fantasy, an image of a better life which is nevertheless revealed as flat, a glossy illusion, separate from the three-dimensional reality of what they are actually doing. This reality returns in Victor's description of their coupling as "two perfect machines doing a job we're designed for" (255); this, despite the admiration for their physical performance, reduces them to mere bodies, evacuating any sense of human sensitivity or soul. There is a comparable moment when Victor describes a woman on top of him as "Pistoning up and then slamming down" (15), with the first action word characterizing their sex as machine-like, and the second suggesting that its energy verges on violence. Victor also thinks of his desire to "bone, shaft, drill, core, screw" women, identifying these words as "euphemisms that aren't" (163). Not merely substitutes for more offensive terms, these words actually capture the brute physicality of sex as Victor sees it, along with an undercurrent of violent rage. Even though Victor may be using these casual encounters as a "sexual anesthetic" (69) to dull the pain that real love might bring—"To keep from feeling anything, I just keep stuffing it" (210)—they only leave him feeling even more lonely as well as viciously angry at his partners for not fulfilling his real needs: "the moment this is over, we'll hate each other," he says about one woman he is with (20), and his friend Denny tells Victor, "You always hate the whole world after you get laid" (100).

But then Victor meets Paige Marshall, who he thinks is his mother's doctor, and his relationship with this woman is different. Although he tries to have unfeeling sex with her, even to take her on the altar of the hospital's chapel, he finds that Paige "seems to be above getting boned" (74). Insofar as this means that Victor does not want to degrade her to the level of a sex object in a merely physical act, it is a good sign, as he realizes: "I didn't want her to become just another piece of ass" (164). However, the fact that Victor finds himself impotent with her is a problem: splitting off the spiritual from the physical, he puts her up on a pedestal as a Madonna figure. He can feel affection for her, as he does for Ida, but he could no more have intercourse with Paige than he could with his mother. In Victor's own description of his Madonna/whore complex, "until your mom dies it seems like all the other women in your life can never be more than just your mistress" (15). Paige herself gives good advice on healing this split when she suggests to Victor, "Maybe sex and affection aren't mutually exclusive" (166). When Paige tells him that "I need you to put your faith in me" (91) as the two of them try to couple on the chapel altar, her words could encourage him to see sex as sacred.

Of course, it is also possible to hear them as a kind of crazed blasphemy, and Paige is in fact a mental patient, not a doctor, in this hospital. Like Ida's, Paige's words and behavior frequently border on lunacy, yet there often seems to be a method to her madness. In her guise as a doctor, Paige advises Victor to impregnate her so that she can use the cells from the fetus to do a neural graft that will restore his mother's mind. It is worth noting that this advice once again brings together sex and affection: if Victor cares about his mother, he should make love with Paige. Victor objects to the entire idea, stating that he does not want to "Kill the unborn to save the elderly" (124). Besides making an argument against abortion, Victor may also be feeling that he has sacrificed enough for his mother, whose smothering closeness and serial abandonment left him "unborn" in the sense of being unable to live his own life. Paige's rebuttal picks up on this personal element in claiming that Victor does not want to go through with her plan because he "can't deal with strong women" like her or his mother and that, "if [his mother] dies, then [his] issue about her will also" (117). Paige has a point: Victor far prefers to deal with women as sex objects than as willful individuals like himself, and he does seem prone to take the despairing view that death will take care of his unresolved issues.

Paige also claims to have translated the diary of Victor's mother as supposedly saying that he was conceived using genetic material from Jesus's foreskin, which would make him the Second Coming of Christ. On the one hand, Paige's "news" encourages Victor to care about others and empowers him to think he can help them, even if doing so requires some self-sacrifice. She has noted approvingly how he aids Alzheimer's patients by accepting the blame for past crimes against them that he never committed, just so that their suffering can find resolution. On the other hand, Paige's encouragement works only too well, for it gives Victor a savior complex that distances him further from common humanity. When she then refuses to have sex with him, saying that it is because he really could be the "divine son of God" (229), she may be teasing him as a way to bring him back to an awareness of his physical needs and his fleshly nature. However, Victor has gone from a despairing emphasis on the mortal body to a grandiose sense of the power of his spirit, without having found a way to combine the two extremes. Before, he seemed resigned to his mother's being moved to the hospital wing reserved for end-stage patients, but now he rushes to her room, claiming that "I'm Jesus Christ" (268) and that "I'm here to save you" (269). Puffed up with pride in his messianic mission, Victor is then horribly deflated when his mother chokes and dies on the chocolate pudding he was feeding her to keep her alive. This is also the moment when he first sees Paige's hospital bracelet and realizes that she is a patient, not a doctor. These shocking realities lead Victor to lose all self-confidence and to discount all of Paige's advice: "My mom's dead, and Paige Marshall is a lunatic" (271); "I'm not anybody's savior" (272).

Yet Paige's advice is not invalidated by Victor's attitudes or actions, for he did not really follow it. While her words pointed him toward a unified view of the spirit and the flesh, of expansive hope and mortal limitations, he has instead vacillated between two extremes, feeling messianic and miserable by turns. Much the same can be said about the way Victor received his mother's advice, which, like Paige's, he tended to take to extremes rather than trying to comprehend it as a unified whole. When Victor was a boy, Ida eschewed a conventional education, saying instead that she wanted him to "know more than just what people think it is safe to tell" him (97). She taught him how to decode innocuous-sounding public announcements made at schools, airports, and hotels so that he could realize their hidden meaning and be safe from crazed gunmen and anthrax attacks.

But, perhaps understandably, young Victor experienced this alternative education as deeply unsettling, making him feel less rather than more secure. Now doom seemed to lurk behind every corner, mortal danger beneath each apparently appealing exterior. Thus, when he as an adult goes to a strip bar and the dancers show him some skin, all Victor can see are moles that could turn cancerous. While working at a historical theme park, Victor reveals hidden truths about the past to visiting schoolchildren, telling how boys used to be exploited as chimney sweeps and got scrotal cancer from the soot. Victor is scaring future generations with these terrible truths, much as he felt traumatized by Ida, and it is not clear that he even thinks they could help save these children; rather, he seems merely to be passing on his gloomy view of the world: "After you find out all the things that can go wrong, your life becomes less about living and more about waiting. For cancer. For dementia" (105); "There is no soul. There is no God. There's just . . . disease and death" (156).

It is true that, in her final days, Ida herself lamented having had a negatively critical disposition rather than a more creative one, regretting that "I fought *against* everything, but . . . I was never *for* anything" (111). Yet Ida's advice to young Victor had in fact contained explicitly positive elements, which he initially overlooked in his tendency to blame all his troubles on his mother. Only now does he remember that she had told him not just to look for the hidden dangers lurking within things that may seem safe, but also to try to view those things as they are, unencumbered by crippling anxiety or fear. For example, she encouraged him to see a mountain as a mountain, "without thinking of logging and ski resorts and avalanches" (149). If, instead of seeing deforestation and commercialism and natural disasters, he could just view the mountain as itself, then it would not seem foredoomed. Possibilities for it to escape the usual fate of mountains would open up, and Victor, no longer bound by negative past precedent, could help to invent those positive possibilities. On one of their trips together, Ida threw away the official map and had Victor draw his own of the mountains up ahead, naming them himself with new words that had different meanings from the ones already assigned by society: "my mom told me that I could reinvent the whole world. That I had that kind of power. That I didn't have to accept the world the way it stood, all property-lined and micromanaged. I could make it anything I wanted" (280).

Plunged into despair over his failure to save his mother, feeling that the world is foredoomed, Victor recalls Ida's empowering advice at just the right time. If he is not the Messiah, then neither is he fated merely to suffer future misery. Ida's advice was both faulty *and* useful. She alerted him to hidden dangers and made him fearful of the future; she emboldened him with high hopes and burdened him with unrealistic expectations. Recognizing that his mother was both right *and* wrong helps Victor to see that same combination in himself. Hearing Ida express her regrets helps him to forgive her, to remember the good advice she gave, and to try to learn from her and her mistakes. As Palahniuk sums it up, "You can either spend your entire life worrying about all these things that could go wrong, that are somehow festering or about to spring out of nowhere for you, or you can live your life about something entirely different that you want to move towards. That's what I wanted Victor to eventually do, stop worrying about what could happen out of the past, into creating what would happen out of the future."[70] Palahniuk has compared Victor's mother to Tyler and suggested that, unlike Jack, who ends up in a mental institution at the end of *Fight Club,* Victor might be able to take that next step toward building a future: "I wanted to have a Tyler Durden character that tears things down—and that's Ida Mancini—who realizes that her entire life of rebellion and anarchy has been fun, but boy, she never did take that next step of actually standing for something. So I wanted to make Victor the generation that would move beyond attacking constantly to creating something."[71]

And so the last book in Palahniuk's four-novel series about the struggle for personal identity ends with Victor no longer bound by the past but free to create in the present—"creating yourself out of a purpose, out of something you stake your life on, that you commit to."[72] But just what is Victor committed to in the end? What world or self is he creating? If he is able to find a balance between his desire to save people and an awareness of his own limitations, as his mother might have wished, the novel's ending does not show us how. If he is able to combine sex and affection and make love to Paige, we do not see this happen. What we do see is Victor and Paige, without the official sanction of a building permit and without the preset guidelines of any architectural plans, working together to "put one rock on top of another" (292) to create some heretofore unimagined structure: "what we build could be anything" (293).

Critics have had difficulty with this ending. Alex E. Blazer argues that "such redemption, as afforded by the novel's supposedly constructive and hopeful ending, is a sentimental sham as the postmodern subject [Victor] is part unconscious narcissist and part conscious nihilist who believes in nothing, not even himself."[73] Victor *could* slip back into a narcissistic sense of his own omnipotence, but after the shock of his failure to save his mother, such a slippage seems unlikely. A more plausible threat is that he might again succumb to nihilistic despair, but to ward off this danger, he has Paige's love, along with his mother's empowering advice, both of which encourage him to believe in his ability to change the world and reinvent himself.

But to what end? There is still the question of what is represented by the novel's conclusion, in which he and Paige "build a world out of rocks" (292). *New York Times* critic Janet Maslin finds that "The note of hope on which the book ends is touching, but it feels entirely vague and not linked to much that has come before."[74] The ending gains more specificity when we realize that it has a personal significance for Palahniuk, whose "father was a rock collector" and whose "earliest memories are of hunting for agates with him." I would suggest that, as Victor works with Paige to gather rocks and build the structure, he remains connected with his mother, following her advice to create anew, much as Palahniuk, who has compared the "act" of "writing" to the "act of collecting stones and assembling them," remains connected with his father.[75] It is also worth noting that, when he is not writing, Palahniuk works in his garden, where he has "tons of rocks" that he "dragged home and heaped around,"[76] building "partial doorways, walls and windows" as a "living metaphor of his life and work."[77] Palahniuk the author *is* Victor, putting one word on top of another to create his fictional world.

If, minus the personal meaning, the novel's "rock metaphor" ending seems "vague and not linked to much that has come before," that is precisely the point. The rocks Victor builds with are like the mountain that his mother encouraged him to see unencumbered by any past associations. The rocks are rocks, the way the mountain was itself, and just as Ida threw away the official map in order for Victor to draw his own view of the mountain, he and Paige eschew any architect's blueprint so that they are free to build a structure of their own imagining.

CHAPTER 3

The Horror Trilogy

Lullaby, Diary, Haunted

After September 11, 2001, Palahniuk turned away from "'transgressive writing,' where you had people doing illegal things—extreme things—but for noble reasons"[1]—things like hijacking planes (*Survivor*) or plotting to bring down skyscrapers (*Fight Club*). As he noted, after the terrorist attack on the Twin Towers, "my phone was just ringing all day long. People from around the world saying 'Were you responsible for this?'"[2] Writing about violence was being confused with violence itself: "Right now any sort of civil disobedience or cultural terrorism—from [fiction like] *The Monkey Wrench Gang* to *Trainspotting*—is all being lumped together and condemned as terrorism," Palahniuk said, "and so those books are just not being brought out by publishers; publishers are self-censoring."[3]

In a post-9/11 environment less receptive to transgressive fiction—"People won't hear it sympathetically, they won't be able to laugh at it easily"[4]—a more indirect approach to cultural criticism seemed advisable, and so Palahniuk turned to the horror genre as a "more effective avenue for social commentary."[5] His main model was horror novelist Ira Levin, whom he admired for being "so very good at finding aspects of the culture that were predominant during periods of time and creating metaphorical monsters around them."[6] *Rosemary's Baby* (1967), in which a woman is forced to carry the devil's baby, used the trappings of horror to dramatize the female battle for reproductive rights before Roe v. Wade, and *The Stepford Wives* (1972), which has husbands turning their unruly wives into "happy homemaker" robots and sex dolls, anticipated the male backlash against feminism. As Palahniuk said about his goal for the novels in his horror trilogy, "I would really love to come up with some metaphors that nail some social issues that we're too frightened to talk about baldly."[7]

Lullaby

One such issue is the media saturation of our minds. Billboards, newspapers, radio, television, movies, computers, smartphones—the media constantly assail us with messages through multiple devices. Given these corporate attempts to control consciousness, is there any room left for independent thought? From reading the anticonsumerist magazine *Adbusters,* Palahniuk adopted the notion of "mental environmentalism," or "the idea that your mind, that your consciousness is as much an environment as a wetland or a desert or a body of water, and that what you allow into that environment can destroy it. . . . Everywhere we look, we are just bombarded with memes, with these logos and brand names and slogans."[8] According to Palahniuk, "*Lullaby* deals with memes, and the way mass culture can fill your head and leave your mind crippled and unable to imagine or think."[9] In a world overrun by mass media messaging, the words of a mere writer can seem weak by comparison. Indeed, even thinking of those words, formulating alternative modes of thought, can seem impossible. This struggle took on a particular shape for Palahniuk in the person of a neighbor lady who "opens every window and blasts every sunny day with her record collection. Bagpipes, Chinese opera, you name it. Noise pollution. After some days and weeks of her blaring noise," he said, "I could've killed her."[10]

In *Lullaby,* Carl Streator discovers a children's verse or "culling poem" whose words kill people, including an upstairs neighbor who was playing music too loud. The fatal verse helps create a zone of silence in which Streator can hear himself think about something other than what the corporate media have been invading his mind with: "Maybe without Big Brother filling us, people could think. The upside is maybe our minds would become our own."[11] The deadly poem is also Palahniuk's way of imagining a world where he as an author could have some real influence, his words not always drowned out by the mass media: "it would be nice to see words come back into power" (60). But, in having people actually die from words, Palahniuk also critiques the idea of too much power being placed in one person's hands. If his words as a writer could kill, would he be able to keep from abusing that power? It is almost as though, as a thought experiment, Palahniuk is exploring a world in which his words could be terrorist acts, in which fiction could produce fatalities like those of 9/11. If words did have this much power, the temptation to abuse it would be great, and the result could be government-imposed censorship of all forms of communication for fear that any radio broadcast, TV program, song lyric, phone text, or book might contain the fatal verse. "Imagine the books burning," Streator thinks—and here Palahniuk must also be imagining his own transgressive novels going up in flames—"Any new word. Anything they don't already understand will be suspect, dangerous" (42). Thus Palahniuk's authorial desire to have his words make a more direct impact on the world could backfire, provoking a ban on all alternative voices as potentially dangerous, bringing down the very censorship he was trying to oppose.

Ideally, words are different from violent acts. Words can be the vehicle for independent thought, self-expression, communication with others, and the peaceful resolution of conflict. But the fatal verse allows no time to persuade others or to reconsider one's own point of view. Instead, it changes people's minds by obliterating them. When Streator has a problem with someone, he just thinks the words of the poem and that person dies: "by now, killing is a reflex. It's the way I solve everything" (236). Of course, nothing is really "solved" this way; real resolution would require the two parties to talk about and work through their differences. With this idea of a verse that literally causes people to drop dead, Palahniuk is "making fun of how fast we go to death as a resolution. As a culture, we believe that if we kill something, we've killed the issue."[12]

At the time, Palahniuk was struggling with a very personal decision about the value of killing. A man named Dale Shackleford had been convicted of murder for the shooting deaths of Palahniuk's father and the woman he was dating, Shackleford's ex-wife. As Palahniuk has explained, "I was writing *Lullaby* when I was also writing my victim's rights statement. As part of that statement, I had to decide if I favored the death penalty."[13] A death sentence is, in a sense, words that kill, and if Palahniuk recommended one that was carried out, he would share in the responsibility for taking a life. So he had to ask himself, "Should the man who killed my father die? Does that resolve anything for me, will seeing him die make my life any better?"[14]

In *Lullaby,* Streator's thoughts about a character named Nash can be seen as Palahniuk's metaphorical way of thinking about Shackleford. Shackleford had a long history of rape before he was convicted of murder. When Nash gets hold of the fatal verse, he uses it to kill a series of unobtainable women and have sex with their dead bodies. Streator accidentally kills his own wife with the verse by reading it aloud before he realizes it is fatal, and has sex with his wife's still-warm body before realizing she is dead. Streator struggles with the question of whether somewhere deep inside he himself has dark impulses that make him similar to Nash. "You can't kill me," Nash says, "we're exactly alike" (235). Even if they are not exactly alike, would killing Nash be mostly a denial of Streator's own guilt—along with a concomitant refusal to recognize Nash's humanity, even though the man has done terrible things? But Streator also considers whether "killing Nash would be saving him. Returning him to God. Connecting him to humanity by resolving his sins" (236). Palahniuk has had comparable thoughts about seeing Shackleford get the death penalty, pondering whether "the only way to bring the criminal back into humanity is to capture and punish him. His punishment becomes his redemption. It's an act of kindness."[15]

In the end, Palahniuk did use this reason to recommend a death sentence, but his insistence on forcing himself to witness Shackleford's execution bespeaks continuing doubt about the morality of the decision: "there's too much in the world of people wanting things killed but not wanting to be there for it. It's going to be a terrible thing. I think I should suffer the consequences for having brought it about, at least by being present for it."[16] The novel is even more ambivalent about Streator's decision to use the deadly poem to kill Nash. Despite thinking that "killing Nash would be saving him" (236), Streator deploys the lethal poem only when Nash tries to kill *him* and then immediately doubts whether killing really solves anything. Earlier, he had been confronted with the question, "So your answer for too much killing is more killing?" (155). Additionally, Streator believes that he himself now deserves to be punished—executed?—for the killing he has just committed: "He's [Nash is] saved, but I'm not. . . . I sit and wait for the police to save me. To deliver me to God and reunite me with humanity" (237). It is as though, in killing the sinful Nash, Streator believes that he has committed a sin, one for which he too will have to be punished in turn. This is a far cry from feeling that imposing a death sentence on another is entirely justified.

Streator undertakes a search to find and destroy all the books containing the deadly verse. Along the way, he meets Helen Hoover Boyle, who also accidentally killed her own child and spouse before realizing that the poem was lethal. Now Helen is a realtor who deliberately kills clients with the poem in order to facilitate the resale of their houses—and a professional assassin who gets paid in diamonds for deploying the verse to eliminate the people on her hit list. If Streator represents patriarchy or "the entrenched aristocracy," Palahniuk likens the "female character, Helen," to "the bourgeoisie; she's managed to attain a certain amount of power, but she really, really would love to have more. She would love to be in the aristocracy."[17] When Streator describes the green suit Helen is wearing, he does so in a way that indicates her class aspirations while also satirizing them: "It's not the green of an avocado, but more the green of avocado bisque topped with a paper-thin sliver of lemon, served ice cold in a yellow Sèvres soup plate" (82). Later, after Helen is attacked by someone who wants *her* power, the lethal verse, the description changes to emphasize that material possessions cannot protect her from physical pain: "Her face is red. It's not the red of a Burmese ruby. It's more the red of the blood running down from her knees" (185). Finally, when Helen has lost everything in the end, Streator says, "The details of her suit are, it's some color. It's a suit. It's ruined" (251). Language shorn of metaphor stands for Helen stripped of all her bourgeois pretensions to finery.

The character who attacks Helen is Oyster, the boyfriend of her young secretary in the real-estate office, Mona. Palahniuk compares Oyster and Mona to "the proletariat who have no power and are willing to do anything to get some power."[18] Oyster believes that the older generation is ruining the world, that global capitalism is polluting the planet and destroying the "mental environment" with its corporate media, laying waste to all local wildlife and indigenous cultures. Oyster wants to use the poem's killing power to hasten this destruction. "I'm all for wiping the slate clean, of books and people, and starting over," he says (160–61). Oyster's nihilistic belief that environmental devastation is too far gone to stop, that hastening the end of humanity is the only answer, is itself a kind of killing poem, for it is conducive to despair. After hearing Oyster talk about humans introducing invasive plants that overrun the native species, Streator thinks of the boy's words as "a plague you catch through your ears. . . . The virus of his information. What used to be a beautiful deep green jungle to me, it's now a tragedy of English ivy choking everything else to death" (157). From one perspective, the world may be nothing but an endless power struggle with each group striving for dominance over the others, but seeing the world entirely through Oyster's eco-terrorist eyes can take all the joy out of life.

After attacking Helen in a failed attempt to grab the lethal poem from her, Oyster dares her to use it against him. "Go ahead," he says. "You killed your real son. You can kill me" (185). Helen already feels guilty enough about having read the poem to her son before realizing its deadly effect. Oyster's words threaten to fill her with suicidal despair, causing her to feel much more responsible for her child's death than she really was. Helen sounds like Oyster when she says that lullaby readers "just want the child to sleep. They just want to dominate. No matter how much you love someone, you still want to have your own way" (148). This is Helen's guilt talking, taking the harshest possible view of parent-child relations and her own role in her son's death. Helen has kept her son cryogenically frozen in the hope of finding an antidote to the killing poem, a resurrection spell from the same grimoire, or book of spells. But it seems that Helen succumbs to despair, unplugging her son's cryogenic unit and drinking drain cleaner as a form of suicide so as to join him in death. However, it turns out that Oyster, using an occupation spell, has taken over Helen's body and caused her to kill herself. In this way, Palahniuk dramatizes the killing effect of Oyster's nihilistic words, the extent to which they overrun her will to live.

If Helen has reason to fear Oyster's negativity, Streator is suspicious of Helen's terms of endearment. Does she really love him, or is she using a love spell from the grimoire to manipulate and dominate him? The whole idea of true love, marriage, a happy home, and a family has been tainted for Streator. Although he read the poem that killed his wife and daughter before realizing its power, he feels guilty: how much did he want his daughter to stop crying and fall asleep? How badly did he want to have sex with his wife? Streator's habit of injuring himself by stamping barefoot on model houses shows both his self-lacerating guilt and his disillusionment with the American dream. Now, when Helen professes to love him and he is tempted to fall for her, he resists. The tragedy of his past has left him fearing that all relationships are about the struggle for dominance, that true love is merely a cultural myth promoted by those who would manipulate others. "Between television and radio and Helen Hoover Boyle's magic spells, I don't know what I really want anymore" (227), Streator thinks, suspecting that "She's the one planting her little seeds. Colonizing me. Occupying me. The mass media, the culture, everything laying its eggs under my skin" (230). Streator's worst fears appear to be realized when, after he is arrested for killing Nash, Helen occupies the body of a police sergeant and conducts a painful anal-cavity search of Streator. It seems that Helen is here revealed to be an invasive occupier, her "love" a kind of rape.

Yet Streator and Helen have much in common, which could allow for love to grow. Both accidentally killed their children and spouses twenty years ago. Each is struggling to find a way to deal with the guilt, rage, and despair from this past. Each is wounded, physically and emotionally, and is dependent on the other for solace. Streator thinks, "My swollen, infected foot, Helen's crushed, scabby knees from Oyster's attack, there's no way to hide these from each other. It's been twenty years, but here I am, somewhere I'd never dreamed I'd ever be again, and I say, I'm falling in love" (222). Both of them have seen how relationships can devolve into a power struggle, and each suspects the other of wanting to dominate, but this mutual suspicion—when it is openly admitted, along with their other shared vulnerabilities—makes them equals and could form the basis for love: "Holding out my hand, I say, 'Here.' And she takes it. And I don't let go. . . . And we're walking hand in hand" (196).

By the end, Helen's body has been destroyed and she is occupying the police sergeant, so she and Streator "*don't have hot sex anymore*" (259), yet Palahniuk has described this as a "demonstration that relationships can be deep and caring and lifelong, but after a certain point, they just don't have to be sexual."[19] Streator is still prey to doubts, wondering if love is a trick to manipulate him and whether sweet but deadly voices are somehow speaking through Helen in order to dominate him: "*Sometimes I worry that Sarge here is really Oyster pretending to be Helen occupying the Sarge*" (258). Streator cannot know for sure that Helen loves him, that he can bring himself to love again, or that true love is even possible. In keeping these questions open, Palahniuk leaves some room for nihilism and despair. But he also suggests that perhaps love is not a matter of *knowing*. "Maybe this is a love story, maybe not," Streator thinks. "It depends on how much I can believe myself" (6).

Diary

For the second volume in his horror trilogy, Palahniuk chose to try his hand at "conspiracy horror, where one person lives their life, not realizing that the world is manipulating and closing in around them."[20] Misty meets Peter while they are students at art college, and the two marry. He brings her back to his family home on Waytansea Island so that they can take care of his mother, Grace, after his father, Harrow, dies; in fact, Harrow is still alive. Despite her use of birth control, Misty becomes pregnant—Peter has sabotaged her contraceptives—and gives birth to a daughter, Tabbi. Some years later, Misty finds Peter in the garage and almost dead from car exhaust, apparently an attempted suicide. In fact, Harrow tried to murder him in order to keep him from leaving the island with Tabbi.

Now that Peter lies comatose in the hospital, Misty is the sole breadwinner and must work as a table server and chambermaid at the local hotel in order to support Grace and Tabbi. Indeed, all the grand old island families, once quite wealthy, have depleted their fortunes and are now reduced to doing menial labor at the hotel. Worn out from work and suffering from headaches, Misty turns to the island doctor for help, but the herbal remedies and drug injections he gives her actually make her worse. When Misty suffers a minor fall, the doctor insists she wear a cast and confine herself to a bed in the hotel attic. After being told the lie that her daughter Tabbi has drowned, Misty has nothing left. The only relief she can find for her suffering is to paint pictures.

Eventually, Misty realizes that she has been the victim of an elaborate plot—and we realize that Palahniuk's "conspiracy horror" is a metaphor for the way in which the rich can prey upon the less fortunate. Once every hundred years, a young man from Waytansea must lure a woman back to the island. There she is gradually deprived of everything—her spouse, her child, her dignity, and her freedom—until the only outlet she has left is the one they have provided for her: to paint. The pictures she draws can then be sold to restore the wealth of the island elite, and the female painter, all used up in serving their purpose, can be left to die. Misty thus becomes a sacrifice on the altar of the greedy elite, and Palahniuk calls attention to the horror of class warfare, the willingness of some to exploit others for monetary gain. As Misty's blue-collar mom once told her, "all big-money fortunes are based on fooling people and pain."[21]

But the horror is even greater when we realize that Misty has been complicit in the plot against her. Yes, there has been a conspiracy, but Misty has been to some extent willfully blind to it, herself caught up in the belief that wealth brings happiness and that she can gain both by taking her place among the old-money families. While on the island, Misty finds herself adopting their snobbish attitude and despising the tourists from the mainland as "invaders, infidels, crowding in to wreck her way of life, her daughter's childhood. All these outsiders" (235). The disparaging terms Misty uses for these recent arrivals reveal her wish to identify with the island's ruling class. Ever since she was a girl growing up in a trailer park, Misty has drawn pictures of grand houses like those on Waytansea Island, pictures representing the "bourgeois dreams of some poor white trash kid" (8): "All this history and tradition she used to think would keep her safe. Insulate her, forever" (33). As Misty uses her present-day diary to reflect upon her childhood, her language shows her gaining some critical distance from those naive beliefs. When she describes the Waytansea wealth and finery as "everything we're programmed to adore" (82), she is working her way toward a new understanding of how she was brainwashed to believe in materialism as the fulfillment of her dreams. When she writes about "the yearning and idiot need of a poor, lonely kid" (82), she is striving for independence and enlightenment—if only she can get beyond self-blame and self-pity for foolishly letting herself fall victim to the lure of old money.

Although Misty's diary diatribes against her formerly credulous self threaten to doom her to despair, such self-criticism is necessary in order for her to realize both her responsibility for her current plight *and* the potential agency she has to change it. She must move beyond thinking of herself as a pure fool and a helpless victim. As Palahniuk has said, "I don't want an innocent character thrust into the world and they are pushed around by inescapable forces. . . . I want a character who made their bed and have to live with the fact that they made their bed and resolve that." Rather than presenting "a character controlled by circumstances," Palahniuk says that he prefers to write about "a character that is creating their circumstances."[22] Writing her diary is Misty's means of moving herself from victimhood to agency, but first she must get past self-blame—and beyond blaming Peter for her predicament.

Misty certainly has her reasons for the rage with which she lashes out at Peter in her diary. The love he professed was apparently a pretense. By disabling her birth control, he tricked her into getting pregnant so that the island aristocracy could have another heir. "For rich people," her mother had warned her, "the first marriage was just about reproduction" (201). Then he subjected her to the islanders' insistence that she draw paintings that would allow them to regain their wealth. In these ways, Peter used her as a mere vessel for reproducing the elite and their lavish lifestyle. Then, by inhaling car exhaust, he put himself in a comatose state, abandoning her to a life of grueling work as a hotel servant to support her daughter and her mother-in-law. As if that were not enough, Misty comes to find out that, prior to his coma, Peter had scrawled graffiti inside hidden rooms of the mainland houses he was remodeling, crazed rants filled with negativity about her. No wonder she writes about him as a "shit sack" who "never loved her" (207) and about herself as a "normal innocent person who sure as hell deserved a lot better" (3).

Yet, as Misty continues to write, her fury turns more and more to sympathy as she begins to understand that Peter was a sufferer and not just an abuser. Angel, one of the mainlanders with a vandalized house, has Misty move her arm to trace Peter's words on the wall so that she can feel what he felt when he wrote them. She comes to realize that, if Peter hated her, it was because he felt forced to marry her as part of the island ritual whereby a young man must lure a female painter to Waytansea. Peter's real love was Angel, but family obligation required him to court Misty instead. Misty, who has been vengefully jabbing the comatose Peter with the pin of the brooch he gave her during their courtship, begins to understand his reasons for having lied to her about his love. When they were first dating, Peter had worn the brooch as a nipple piercing in the hope that Misty would be repulsed by him; the piercing also displays his suffering at being forced to sacrifice himself and his true desires for the sake of his greedy family. Misty could have heeded the warning, as sharp as the brooch pin that almost sticks her during their date, but instead she is enraptured by the prospect of owning such fine jewelry. If Peter's profession of love for her was false, then so was hers for him: "She didn't love her husband as much as she loved his old jewelry and the dream of living in a big stone house" (231). Complicit in her own duping, Misty was not just an innocent victim, and Peter was more than a mere abuser.

Now, when Misty stabs the hospitalized Peter with the brooch, it is less out of an angry need for him to feel her pain and more due to compassion for his, a desire to communicate through shared suffering. As Misty is jabbed with the doctor's needle, confined to the hotel-attic bed, and even catheterized—so that she can continue painting without a bathroom break—her physical affinity with the comatose Peter grows. As she moves toward understanding and forgiving Peter for his part in the islanders' plot, she also begins to forgive herself for her own complicity. If Peter had been in thrall to the old-money traditions, she too had felt drawn to their allure. And if Peter could attempt to resist, then so could she. Misty discovers that he had been trying to save their daughter Tabbi and escape the island when his father staged the scene in the garage to look like a suicide. Peter had wanted to free Tabbi from inheriting a life of materialist values and classist disdain for blue-collar workers. Fearing retribution from his family, he had expressed his real beliefs only by scrawling messages inside hidden rooms, the way carpenters often left secret signs of their existence in houses they built for the upper classes. One of Peter's messages read, "Tabbi will have a better future if her generation has to fend for itself" (229).

Other graffiti is discovered to have been Peter's attempt to warn everyone about the islanders' plot, and Misty also uncovers secret warnings from previous female victims of that plot—women like herself who had been lured to the island, forced to paint, and then disposed of when they were no longer of any use. Together, these writings help Misty to understand her own predicament and spur her to take action so as not to end up like her comatose husband or her victimized predecessors. Palahniuk has described the theme of *Diary* as one that asks, "How can we communicate across time and stop making the same mistakes over and over?"[23] One answer is to learn from the past, understand one's own present, and act to change the future.

But *Diary* also shows that this is much easier said than done. Misty does break out of the cast on her leg and escape her confinement in the hotel attic. Then, using some of Peter's own words, she does warn the visitors from the mainland not to let themselves be used by the Waytansea elite as part of a plot to get rich at others' expense. Thinking that if she prevents the visitors from buying her paintings, she will foil the plot, Misty tells the assembled guests in the hotel dining room not to view her art. But they do, and as they stand there so entranced they are unable to move, the elite burn them alive by setting fire to the hotel. The visitors are enthralled by Misty's paintings of the grand old houses on Waytansea Island in the same way that she used to be lured by their lavish lifestyle. The fiery deaths are a metaphor for the danger of succumbing to that lure, of believing that materialism leads to fulfillment when in fact it is an empty promise. Rather than attaining wealth or happiness, the visitors are merely used by the Waytansea elite to restore their fortune. Insurance from the fire—combined with blackmail money from corporations who pay so that their names will not be linked to the disaster—allows the island aristocracy to regain their wealth and to reassert their disdain for "lower-class" outsiders. Not only are the visitors killed, but Tabbi has joined the island elite and plans to spend the rest of her life with them. In fact, it was she who set fire to the hotel, so Misty cannot tell the authorities about the islanders' plot against the visitors and herself unless she wants to see her own daughter arrested.

Misty seems caught in a vicious cycle whereby, once every hundred years, someone like her is entrapped by the lure of old money, her dreams exploited by the islanders to regain their fortunes at a terrible cost to her and others. It is worth noting that the island elite are themselves also trapped, cut off from the larger world by their classist disdain for "outsiders" and self-doomed to a life of exploiting others in order to shore up fortunes that do not bring happiness:

"Instead of progress, the island was stuck in this repeating loop. Recycling the same ancient success. Period revival. This same ritual" (207). Misty fails to free her daughter from this cycle, to "give Tabbi something better than a future of no challenges" among the idle elite (235), and Misty fails to save herself from being used by the islanders to fill their coffers once again. Thus, in addition to being "conspiracy horror," *Diary* also seems to be an example of "cycle horror," which Palahniuk has defined as a narrative in which "an innocent person happens upon what looks like a bright new beginning, a fresh start, and an escape from the misery of the world. The victim flees to this sanctuary, then discovers it's a trap and this entire new reality has been organized to destroy victims as a means of perpetuating itself."[24] The horror of a cycle narrative lies in its sense of perpetual misery, of inescapable doom: "you can imagine that same cycle or process stretching into the past or future, destroying an endless chain of similar people, all of them denying the dire nature of their circumstances until their fate is inevitable."[25] Misty's entrapment within the islanders' plot, her failure to save herself from their greedy designs, would seem to indicate that she is just another victim in line with her predecessors and the unfortunate women to follow.

However, we have heard Palahniuk say that he is not interested in innocents who fall victim to their circumstances: "I don't believe in that innocent character." Instead, he wants to write about characters "creating their circumstances."[26] *Diary* first began as a kind of haunted-house novel in which each couple that moved in, despite warning signs about the evil that befell previous inhabitants, seemed doomed to the same bad end as their predecessors. As Palahniuk noted, the book "wasn't even about a character. It was about a house"—a house that possessed its occupants so that "their lives went to hell."[27] But to invest a house or any *thing* with this kind of determining power is a denial of human responsibility and agency. Blaming the house for life's disasters makes them seem as fixed and unchangeable as a thing. Palahniuk eventually began to see that his real interest was in human denial rather than haunted houses, in characters like Misty who, despite all signs to the contrary, foolishly believe that a dream home will solve all their problems: "The wish list of a white trash girl: big houses, church weddings" (130). Then, when disaster results, they blame the house rather than realizing their own complicity, the unrealistic expectations and materialistic values that contributed to their bad end. "The book," Palahniuk recognized, "was really about unexamined inspiration—the dreams of childhood, carried into adulthood—and the disasters that happen when we're unaware of the past."[28]

Blinded by her foolish dreams and then incapacitated by her tendency to blame Peter, Misty took too long to come to an understanding of her own responsibility for her plight and her own potential for agency. Eventually, by deciphering the warning messages left by Peter and her female predecessors and by writing about herself in her diary, Misty achieved this understanding, but when she finally acted, it was too late to save the tourists from dying in the fire or to save her daughter from joining the island elite. Yet Palahniuk is unwilling to leave Misty as a mere victim of inescapable fate. If reading and writing could help her break through denial to comprehend her predicament and take positive action, albeit too late, then perhaps the next woman will be smart enough to learn from Misty's past mistakes and act while there is still time to foil the islanders' plot. Of course, there is the very real possibility that the next in line will fail as Misty did. As Palahniuk has observed about characters in "cycle horror" fiction and film, "the victims never get very smart in a cycle story. But the viewers get smart. . . . In a way, the victim dies for the viewer to find enlightenment. . . . People watching cycle stories are people who learn from history."[29]

Misty's story ends when she sends her diary to Palahniuk to be published as the book *Diary*. She hopes that, years hence, some girl—like her former "little trailer park idiot" self (49)—will read it and resist the allure of old jewelry and big houses, the empty promise and fatal trap laid by the elite: "I hope this story will save her—that little girl" (261). By collapsing the characters *in* his book and the readers *of* his book, by suggesting that the next Misty might read *Diary,* Palahniuk creates a productive ambiguity and brings innovation to the "cycle horror" story. Not only might readers of the book learn from Misty's diary, much as she learned from the messages left for her by previous women, but it is possible that a character *in* the book—the next Misty—might also learn from it and act in time to break the vicious cycle. Thus Palahniuk not only gestures toward the positive effect he hopes his words will have, he also refuses the inescapable conclusion of most "cycle horror" stories, the sense of characters doomed to repeat the same miserable fate. By investing responsibility and agency in people rather than blaming houses or things, by writing about characters with the potential for "creating their circumstances," he escapes from the confines of the "cycle horror" genre and invents his own kind of fiction.

Haunted

On book tours to promote *Diary,* Palahniuk would read his short story "Guts" and people in the audience would faint. In city after city, bookstore after bookstore, audience members would break into a sweat, groan, and drop to the floor. Had the author devised a true-life version of *Lullaby*'s fatal verse—words with an almost deadly impact on their listeners? Was the point of the story merely to create this sensational effect, this effect on the senses, as a publicity event to drum up interest in Palahniuk's work? He did admit to having been inspired by Shirley Jackson's horror story "The Lottery," which, when it first appeared in the *New Yorker*, provoked a number of readers to cancel their subscriptions to the magazine: "before I sat down to write 'Guts,' I thought, how would you have to write 'The Lottery' now, in such a way that you'd generate that same strong outrage?"[30] And yes, Palahniuk was pleased that, in a world where books are often overshadowed by other media, his fiction produced a marked effect. "I'm always proud when spoken words from a story can have any kind of physical impact," he said.[31]

But there is more to the physical impact of "Guts" than mere sensationalism or public outrage. In writing the story, Palahniuk used the technique he learned from Tom Spanbauer's writers' workshop called "going on the body." This technique involves describing a "physical sensation" in such a way that it can "evoke a sympathetic physical sensation from the reader": "the goal is to make the story occur in the reader's mind, heart and gut."[32] "Guts" is the story of a thirteen-year-old boy who, while sitting at the bottom of a pool and using its suction pump as a masturbation aid, has part of his large intestine sucked into the drain. The boy is at first unsure of what has happened, believing himself attacked by a snake from below, but when he notices food from a recent meal—"Knotted inside the snake, you can see corn and peanuts"[33]—he realizes to his horror that he is looking at his own prolapsed digestive tract. According to Palahniuk, on his book tours "people fell the moment I read the words 'corn and peanuts.' It was that detail that made seated people go limp" and faint to the floor.[34]

What is of value to Palahniuk is his listeners' sympathetic physical response to the boy's plight, their "gut feeling" a kind of match to his, a shared bodily sense of how terrible this would be if it were happening to them. Palahniuk hints at his desire for this kind of response right from the beginning when the narrator says, "This story should last about as long as you can hold your breath, and then just a little bit longer" (12). At the end of the story, after the narrator is barely able to hold his breath long enough to bite through his own intestine to avoid drowning in the pool, he tells us, "Now you can take a good, deep breath. Because I still have not" (21). The audience has held its breath in suspense with him to the point where some listeners have passed out.

Not only is there a sympathetic connection between the fainting listeners and the suffering character, there is also a greater compassion among the audience members themselves as they care for anyone who has fallen: "Everything stops, and the person who has passed out is the center of everyone's attention. . . . Everyone is focused on and concerned about this one person who's on the floor, unaware. This person is gently served and catered to until they come back to life, resurrected."[35] For Palahniuk, what he calls "the 'Guts' effect" is less about making people fall than it is about seeing them rise again. It has less to do with isolated pain than with bringing people together through compassion for shared suffering. About his readings, Palahniuk has said, "people walked into the event, it was so goddamned crowded, they were shoulder to shoulder, and they hated each other because there was too many other people. But after they had lived through 'Guts,' they were bonded—like they had lived through a major life event. They were laughing, they were high, they were euphoric and they cared for the people who fell down on the ground."[36]

Palahniuk's reading of "Guts" in front of sympathetic audiences stands as a marked contrast to the silent shame that the boy within the story is forced to undergo. Finding that his parents are as disgusted by his masturbatory practices as by the pool accident, the boy is told that the entire incident is never to be discussed. As a result of this enforced silence, the boy not only grows up with a chronic sense of shame, he also suffers from fears due to ignorance, such as believing that his self-pleasuring in the pool is responsible for his sister's pregnancy and subsequent abortion. If his parents had been willing to talk, they could have dispelled such foolish notions and saved him from a lifetime of self-blame.

But that boy, now an adult known as Saint Gut-Free, does finally get to tell his story, which he writes and reads to other aspiring authors at a retreat. He and these authors are the characters in Palahniuk's *Haunted,* which contains "Guts" as one of its twenty-three stories and which has, as its linking narrative, the ongoing tale of this writers' retreat. As Saint Gut-Free recites his story, he folds in embarrassing and hushed-up incidents from the sexual lives of other teenage boys, and thereby begins to feel less isolated in his shame: "The wax kid and the carrot kid are different people, but we all live pretty much the same life" (15). "You digest and absorb your life by turning it into stories," says Mr. Whittier, the organizer of the writers' retreat. "Other events—the ones you can't digest—they poison you. Those worst parts of your life, those moments you can't talk about, they rot you from the inside out" (380).

As a result of his pool accident, Saint Gut-Free had to have a radical bowel resectioning and lost most of his digestive capability. This loss is a metaphor for the silence imposed upon him, the fear that some of his deeds were "Too low to even get talked about" (13). Now, in writing and sharing his story with others, Saint Gut-Free has the chance to revise his former understanding of himself as an isolated "pervert" and to gain the sympathy he never got from his parents. Similarly, Palahniuk finds that, after he gives readings, "the stragglers [in the audience] come up to me and say, 'I need to tell you a story I have never told anyone.' And they nearly always tell me a horrific childhood sexual story. By reading 'Guts,' I've shown them that you can use these awful things that happened to you rather than be used by them."[37] Palahniuk has spoken movingly of "Our need to turn even the darkest parts of life—especially the darkest parts—into stories . . . our need to tell these stories to our peers . . . and our need to be heard, forgiven and accepted by our community."[38]

As the characters in *Haunted* read their stories to the other members of the writers' retreat, they have the opportunity to free themselves from past shame and guilt and to make new lives for themselves in the company of sympathetic listeners. The writers' retreat could function like the close-knit and compassionate writers' group with whom Palahniuk has met since 1991 and to whom he actually read all the stories in *Haunted*: "There we share and discuss our work. We've shared divorces, bankruptcies, newborns, illnesses, and triumphs. . . . The past 20 years supporting each other has been rather . . . epic."[39] Another model for the writers' retreat in *Haunted* is the Landmark Forum, a personal development seminar that Palahniuk attended in 1988. Crediting this experience as "a big epiphany moment," Palahniuk has said that "I was 26 when I did the seminar, convinced the world was out to burn me at every turn. If it wasn't for that seminar, I wouldn't be a writer. They taught me to see how closed down I was, to face my fears."[40] Many of the ideas that Palahniuk learned from the Landmark Forum could be of benefit to the characters in *Haunted,* but their writers' retreat turns out to be a kind of anti–Landmark Forum wherein the participants fail to achieve the epiphanies their stories could have led them to realize, just as they fail to support each other in the ways that a true writers' group would have done.

The character known as Miss America tells a story about punishing her body with relentless exercise in order to lose weight. She is never satisfied with her physique, always fearing that it is not thin enough to look good on camera, since she wants to star in infomercials for an exercise wheel. When she says, "I'm always looking . . . for what's NOT to like" (46), Miss America seems close to understanding how she has trapped herself in an endless search for the ideal body image—a phantom ideal defined by others and not true to herself. This wisdom would be in keeping with the advice of Landmark leaders, who argue, "Every time we opt for *looking good* or *avoiding looking bad* over what's actually true for us, inauthenticity creeps in and we compromise who we are."[41] However, Miss America not only brings her exercise wheel to the writers' retreat where she continues her maniacal workouts, she also engages in vicious competition with the other writers for fame, much as she used to compete with rivals for television spots. She has not learned from the story of her own past. Another character, Mrs. Clark, tells of the time when she and her husband made an amateur porn video. The initial voyeuristic excitement of watching themselves being watched by other couples gave way to a hypercritical sense that their own bodies looked far worse on video than they had imagined they would. But, rather than learning from this disparity to appreciate themselves as they are, the Clarks succumbed to despair over their own physical ugliness, as measured against some fantasized ideal.

Mrs. Clark also tells the story of her daughter, Cassandra, who looks into a Nightmare Box and then loses all interest in her former life of keeping up a fashionable appearance and striving for social advancement. Unlike her mother, who is "addicted to conflict" (313), Cassandra will "never need drama or joy or pain ever again" (347). Having realized the superficiality of what most of society takes to be important, Cassandra has in a sense been reduced to nothingness—a frightening condition because she no longer accepts any of the usual reasons for living. One potential sign of hope is when she says about this nothingness that "It made me want to be a writer" (347), as if reflecting on her experience in words might enable her to understand it and create new reasons for being. Landmark seminars also advise us to get rid of "all the meaning the drama-loving human race applies to things" so that we can reach a state of "no issues, no fear, no expectations for the future."[42] They suggest that we move beyond "a view of ourselves that we essentially just accept" in order to "encounter *nothing* as a freedom," and they advise that "it is in language that the power to choose and the power to create possibility reside."[43]

As for Mrs. Clark, she is too afraid to look inside the Nightmare Box, to confront the nothingness of society's received ideas. Unable to countenance the thought that her daughter may have had a radical insight into the essential meaninglessness of society life, Mrs. Clark maintains that Cassandra must have been the victim of some villainous attack that destroyed her mind. When no villain is forthcoming, Mrs. Clark kills her daughter with an overdose of sleeping pills and afterward returns to the place where she left the body—not in order to confess her guilt but instead to declare that she was justified in taking Cassandra's life. Rather than admit the deeper truth of Cassandra's insight, Mrs. Clark sticks to her own story of her daughter's having been so victimized that she is better off dead. Thus Mrs. Clark fails to learn from the tale she tells. She becomes like a "killer" who returns to the scene of the crime to "convince himself with the story of his" reality: "The reality that—he was right" (137). Such a self-righteous insistence on one's own version of reality is something that Landmark warns against. As one seminar leader put it, "We make others wrong so we can be right and you just love to be right, don't you?"[44]

Comrade Snarky recounts the tale of her women's support group and what happened when a stranger named Miranda tried to join it. Several of the women had been subjected to molestation or rape by men in the past, so the arrival of Miranda, who is suspected of being a male-to-female transsexual, makes them feel unsafe. In their fear of any possible recurrence of male violence, the women do not accept Miranda's statement that "he" was born female. Acting on this fear and also in unconscious revenge for past wrongs done to them by men, the women humiliate Miranda, grab at "his" female breasts, poke at "his" vagina, and eventually force "his" legs apart in order to prove with a flashlight that "he" is really a man. It is left unclear what, if anything, they thereby discover, but in the process of attempting to prove themselves right, the women enact the very violation they had wanted to avoid seeing repeated. Rather than helping them to acknowledge and move beyond former trauma through their consciousness-raising sessions, the stories they tell each other about past male violence have led to increasing fear and suspicion, resulting in further violent acts. "Contexts come to define us by default, and we live our lives essentially unaware of their existence and of their far-reaching influence," Landmark leaders warn. They advise "becoming aware of and responsible for *whatever* context we are functioning inside of, and realizing that we have the power not only to invent contexts, but to move freely among them."[45] By contrast, the women allow the past to become the determining context for their present actions.

They are also so busy blaming "males" like Miranda for having victimized them that they fail to recognize their own villainy. Like the women's group, the characters at the writers' retreat maintain that "There are *victims*" and "there are *villains*," and that one should not "create shades of gray that a mass audience can't follow" (209). However, the goal of Palahniuk's horror fiction is to explore these shades of gray, to present the kind of "monster" in which "the villain and the victim are the same person." By combining the two, he hopes to "remind people that we create most of our own problems."[46] A character called the Matchmaker tells a wartime story about an enemy officer who forces a female prisoner to give him oral sex. During the act, he slits her throat, but in the process also severs his own male member. Through this physical connection with her, he is made to feel his own vulnerability, but any potential sympathy that their shared suffering might lead him to have for her is fleeting, for they both die from his knife. Nevertheless, the Matchmaker could learn from this story of a villain who, in victimizing the other, becomes a victim himself. But he does not; instead, he plans to chop off his own penis, while blaming someone else, so that he will have a horrific survival tale that he can sell to the media. Instead of learning from the past, the Matchmaker repeats it. Always blaming others, failing to see his own villainy, he does become a victim—of himself.

Then there is the Missing Link, a Native American character who tells about the time when Mandy, a female anthropology student, dated him in order to gather evidence for her theory that members of his tribe sometimes turn into ravenous werewolves. Mandy's theory is an offensive stereotype that reduces nonwhite males to lustful—sexually hungry—bodies, as when she says that "Chewlah men all have a big dick and balls for their face" (298). It is Mandy who is the predator in this tale, so hungry for fame that she offers him oral sex if he will prove her theory, but instead of maintaining his human dignity, the Missing Link decides to conform to her stereotype of him as a beast. In order to "get a piece of ass" (306), he makes her his sexual and murderous prey. It is as though, rather than *using* Mandy's "horror story" of Native Americans as werewolves, he has let himself *be used* by it. Rather than gaining an awareness of the context in which she has placed him so that he can realize his power to invent new ones, the Missing Link allows that context to determine his actions. It comes as no surprise, then, that at the writers' retreat the Missing Link dies from choking on the Matchmaker's severed penis, which he has attempted to eat so that he can achieve media fame with the most awful survival tale. From being the victim of Mandy's hunger for fame, the Missing Link has gone on to become a predatory villain like her—one who ultimately ends up victimizing himself.

Palahniuk has described the meetings of his own writers' group as a form of "talk therapy"[47] where the members tell often horribly painful, deeply personal stories, acknowledge the extent to which they are responsible for and not just victims of the past, and seek understanding and forgiveness from each other. As a result, participants learn that they can "control the story" rather than be controlled by it; they can attain "some sense of power over the pain"[48] by realizing that they are not doomed to repeat the past but instead can create new possibilities. By contrast, the characters at the writers' retreat in *Haunted* tell stories in a way that extends and exacerbates the pain of the past. Rather than admit that their stories are sometimes embarrassing or self-incriminating, these writers tell self-righteous tales to make themselves look good or to claim that they are the victims of villainous others. Where bonds could form based on shared physical suffering, these characters engage in blaming and backstabbing as a desperate attempt to deal with their fears of vulnerability and mortality. "People fall so in love with their pain, they can't leave it behind," one character says. "The same as the stories they tell. We trap ourselves" (380). Rather than exorcise their fears, the stories these characters tell only make them feel more haunted.

CHAPTER 4

Teen Terrors

Rant, Pygmy

After his foray into horror fiction, Palahniuk turned to science fiction with *Rant,* a novel originally intended to be the first in a trilogy but which so far stands alone. As with horror, science fiction became the means by which he could present a social critique while cloaking it in the guise of a popular genre, thus making it seem less flagrantly controversial in a political environment inhospitable to transgressive fiction. However, by the time of *Pygmy* two years later (2009), Palahniuk apparently felt that he could once again deal more directly with incendiary themes, for this novel depicts a sleeper cell of teenage terrorists who have infiltrated small-town America as foreign-exchange students and who plan to spread a deadly neurotoxin. True to his belief that transgressive fiction would not have to remain underground forever—"that won't always be the case, the farther we get from 9/11"[1]—Palahniuk returns in *Pygmy* to the more openly confrontational writing for which he became known in the 1990s. I have paired *Rant* and *Pygmy* because the former novel's titular character is also a kind of teen terror in that he spreads rabies, causing an epidemic. Moreover, the antiheroes of both novels struggle to define their own identities against the views constantly being projected upon them by surrounding characters.

Rant

As a baby, Rant was his mother Irene's little angel, almost feminine with his long eyelashes and pink cheeks. But when she sees the blobs of dried snot he has stuck on his bedroom wall, she calls him a monster. Palahniuk compares the snot to "a little black fingerprint," suggesting that it is the assertion of Rant's own identity that really upsets Irene, as all mothers are disturbed when they are no longer "one person with their child."[2] Later, when Rant is a child dyeing Easter eggs under his mother's tutelage, his father, Chester, chides her for feminizing him: "Don't ruin the boy for getting married" (40). When Rant is bitten by a black-widow spider while hunting for Easter eggs in his mother's garden, Chester insists that the tearful boy find all the eggs before getting medical treatment. Chester thus pressures him to toughen up and be a man, while Irene has tried to influence their son to be sensitive and artistic. Rant rebels against both his parents' attempts to determine his destiny. He disappoints his mother by coloring the Easter eggs to resemble grenades, but he gets back at his father by planting the rotten-egg "grenades" in the grass so that they explode as stink bombs on Chester when he mows the lawn.

Rant tries to make his own way in life, steering between feminine and masculine influences. Much as his father might wish, Rant continues to stick his hand down holes in the ground in order to be bitten by animals, toughening himself up against whatever unknown pain the future may bring. Before going to school, he also secretly discards the fancy clothes his mother has embroidered for him. However, this is less because he wants to avoid being thought a sissy than out of sympathy for his mother's feelings, not wanting her to be ridiculed by the other kids for her amateurish artistic efforts. As a teenager, Rant shows sensitivity during oral sex when he takes the time to really taste and know the girls he sleeps with, much as his mother always insisted that everyone chew slowly to appreciate the food she prepared. And yet, along with giving them "feminine" sympathy, Rant also acts like an intrusive male by infecting these girls with disease, spreading the rabies he contracted from the bites.

Rant's openness to sensory experience, his acute awareness of taste and smell, is sometimes coded as feminine, but at other times it seems more animal, as if beyond or before social categories of gender and sexuality. Often likened to a werewolf or a pet dog that has gone wild to run with the wolves, rabid Rant can identify the male and female owners of discarded condoms and tampons from their smell. Conventional society fears him because he does not fit its desired definitions: "A sexually conflicted thirteen-year-old rattlesnake-venom junkie with rabies—well, it's safe to say that's every father's worst nightmare" (75). When Rant has his photo taken kissing a boy, he knows that his parents will think worse of him as a result, but he hopes that this will help them miss him less when he is gone. Another man, witnessing the kiss, begins to call Rant "Huckleberry Fagg" (151). Significantly, Palahniuk has described Rant as "an updated American archetype, Huckleberry Finn or Tom Sawyer or Thoreau, this half-human but half-animal person, who lives a sort of animal awareness in that he is always really present and aware of what he's doing at any moment. He's not interpreting the present through the past or he's not interpreting the present in anticipation of the future." Rant may be "kind of slow seeming," uncultured and uncivilized, but he is "also just really immediately physical."[3] For example, when Rant sticks his hand into a ground hole, he experiences empathy for the animal he touches, reaching "to feel that fur and the rattle of a fast heartbeat underneath. That heartbeat almost as fast as" his (68). Rant's deformed girlfriend Echo falls for him after she sees how gently he treats a spider, one that "looks as ugly as" she feels herself to be (181).

Rant's physical feeling for others is in stark contrast to the egotistical indifference of a character named Green Taylor Simms. Simms has been traveling back in time in order to mate with his own female ancestors, including his mother, Irene. Despite his claim that the women are willing and excited to receive him, Irene's account of the sex he has with her when she is thirteen makes it clear that his advances constitute forcible as well as statutory rape. The experience for her is bewildering and painful. At first she thinks that he has covered her with his body in order to protect her from some wild dogs. She believes that both of them must be feeling a shared sense of present danger, so when the dogs are gone, she assures him, "We're safe" (281). But Simms proceeds to violate her—twice, so that he can be sure his seed is implanted. "To be safe," he says, "we'll need to go again" (282). Her idea of "safety" is communal and present-tense; his is selfish and future-oriented. He is only mating with her in order to stoke his own genes, for every time he conceives with an ancestor, he will feel stronger and more alive. Simms ignores her frightened heartbeat; his is slow and steady. He uses his heightened senses only to detect when she had her last period so that he can be sure she is ovulating and fertile for his seed. He is indifferent to the suffocating weight and stabbing pain that she feels during the rape.

Not only does Simms go back in time to fortify himself by mating with his ancestors, he also uses his foreknowledge of the future to make money, thereby enriching himself. Once Simms has acquired enough strength and wealth, he decides to make himself immortal by killing his ancestors, for without them he would be like a god, outside of time with no beginning or end. The child that Simms conceives with Irene is Chester. When Chester has grown to be a young man, Simms asks him to go back in time to kill Irene, but instead Chester attempts to save her from the assault by Simms. Arrayed against Simms's destructive egotism, Chester offers a saving empathy for his mother's suffering. However, he is too late, arriving just after the rape has occurred. All he can do is comfort her in the wake of the attack, helping his mother to clothe herself again against the cold weather, even as she offers him her sweater to keep warm. Chester's compassion forms a marked contrast to Simms's callousness.

Chester feels Irene's present fear and pain, whereas Simms was only using her as a kind of depository to fortify his future. Chester marries Irene so that he can keep watch against further attacks by Simms.

Rant, who grows up thinking that Chester is his father, is the child conceived when Simms time-travels again to sire another child upon Irene. Once Rant has grown to be a young man, Simms asks him to go back in time to kill Irene, promising him money and immortality if he does so. Since Rant is the product of Simms's mating with his own mother, Rant, like Chester, is a version of Simms; all three appear identical and have the same DNA. When Simms offers lucre and everlasting life to Rant, he is really deeding these to himself.

However, like Chester, Rant refuses to assert his own ego in dominance over his mother. Simms raped her, as if he could bring himself into the world as an entirely self-made man, and now he wants her dead so that he can sever all ties with his maternal origins and become immortal. By taking all the life and hoarding all the money from the present, Simms hopes to become a god in the future.

But Rant looks for a way to define himself that does not involve denying others. Behind the dried snot he stuck to his bedroom wall, the "fingerprints" of himself that so upset his mother, he has hidden gold coins *for her.* Rant asserts himself by giving rather than hoarding; he defines his own identity by reaching out to others, the way he reached down into the ground holes to feel the animals' hearts beating like his own. Simms, a child rapist and serial killer, ruins the present-day lives of his female ancestors, impregnating or murdering them so that he will have a better future. By contrast, Rant's sensory awareness in the present alerts him to others' suffering, which is like his own, and prompts him to try to save them and himself, which is why he refuses Simms's bribe of an omnipotent future and goes back in time to prevent Simms's assault on his mother.

It is unclear whether Rant succeeds. There is some suggestion that, arriving too late to stop the rape and conception of another Simms child, Rant changes his name to Chester and acts as a father to the new Rant until *he* is old enough to go back in time to try to stop the rape and conception of another Simms child. Repeated failures on Rant's part could lead to endless "backward loops in time" (286) or what Palahniuk calls "a Moebius strip"[4] in which Rant keeps becoming Chester becoming Rant becoming Chester and never stopping Simms, in which every effort to foil Simms merely ends where it began, with another attempt seemingly foredoomed to failure. But to believe that Rant is foreordained to fail is to believe that the past predetermines the future, without the possibility of an intervening change in the present. Rant refuses to accept that he is merely an extension of Simms, a son who can do nothing but carry out his father's nefarious plot, who is nothing but "the result of somebody's longtime, sick-assed plan" (253). Instead, Rant believes that he can make his own identity in the present. "No matter what happens, it's always now," Rant says (246), and if that is so, then the "future you have tomorrow won't be the same future you had yesterday" (253) because your present actions can alter the course of history and make for a different future. This is why, despite what appears to be an endless loop of failures, Rant continues to try to stop the assault on his mother: there is the ever-present chance that he will succeed, foil the plot that his father has laid out, and thereby create a better future.

The temporal loops and twisted family relations in *Rant* may seem outlandish and far removed from reality, causing the reader to feel like a character in the novel who remarks, "My head's working overtime to swallow the mess of this" (313). Yet it is possible that this science fiction is rooted in the true-life, tragic events of Palahniuk's own family history. As we know, his grandfather murdered his grandmother. Then, before killing himself, the grandfather almost shot Palahniuk's father but could not find the boy, who was hiding under a bed. Many years later, as we have also noted, Palahniuk's father was himself killed by a man with a gun. In referring to these events, Palahniuk has wondered whether there might not be a "pattern" to them, "the shape of this perfect completion of a thing that started so long ago."[5] The author has said that he learned to pronounce his last name when his father took him to see two gravestones, one for his grandmother Paula and the other for his grandfather Nick.[6] Could Palahniuk be concerned about the determining influence of his paternal lineage, about his being doomed to repeat the fate of his forefathers? The novel may figure this concern in the form of "grandfather" Simms who tries to compel "father" Chester and son "Rant" to kill Irene, the "(grand) mother."

Palahniuk has mentioned the time when, as a six-year-old boy, he got a washer stuck on his finger, which turned black, and his father, Fred, threatened to cut it off, actually leading him to a chopping block and raising an ax before deliberately missing. Fred explained that this was to teach the boy that actions—like playing with the washer—have consequences,[7] but an unintended lesson might well have been to instill fear of the father's latent violence. Years later, Fred came to realize that, while he may have blamed his father, Nick, for not being there when Fred was growing up, he himself could rightfully be blamed for the mistakes *he* made as a father to Chuck.[8] Speaking of the "personal issue at the core" of *Rant*, Palahniuk noted that, "after a certain age, every time you look in that bathroom mirror, you are kind of becoming your worst enemy, that is, your dad. . . . I am becoming everything that I did not like about my dad."[9] We recall that Rant, Chester, and Simms all look exactly alike, and the novel takes up the question of whether Chester or Rant will repeat Simms's violence.

Palahniuk has said that, in realizing the extent to which he is "very much like" his father, he also finds himself "having to forgive" his father,[10] much as Fred, in recognizing how much he himself was to blame, had come to a new understanding of his own father Nick's shortcomings. *Rant* is in fact dedicated to Palahniuk's father, Fred. Asked what he would change if he could go back in time, Palahniuk said not only that "I'd stop my mother smoking," thus saving her—from lung cancer—the way that Rant tries to save Irene, but also that "I'd stop . . . my father going on the trip he was on when he was killed."[11] The only way in which Rant can save Chester is by joining him in diverging from Simms's destructive course of action and living a life of compassion for others, as Fred and Chuck tried to depart from the negative example of Nick.

To dramatize Rant's struggle to avoid letting himself be defined by others, Palahniuk wrote *Rant* in the form of an oral biography by multiple narrators, each of whom tries to impose his or her own view of the titular protagonist. For Palahniuk, Rant was "a cipher," "more of a projection of everyone around him,"[12] or as Rant himself puts it, "You're a different human being to everybody you meet" (18). The oral-biography form not only allowed Palahniuk to "cut together information like a film editor" without using the transitional phrases of more conventional fiction; it also enabled him to "juxtapose conflicting or contrasting perceptions about the same event" or character.[13] The government charges that Rant was a superspreader of rabies, but his mother maintains that they have set him up as a patsy for deaths he did not cause.

Some believe that he was merely a political scapegoat for a nonexistent rabies epidemic, a panic created as a pretext to segregate the population into Nighttimers, social misfits and undesirables who are only allowed out at night, and Daytimers, respectable citizens who now have the day hours exclusively to themselves. Palahniuk presents one Daytimer's distanced and condemnatory view of society's "others"—"please consider how Nighttimers live. The rest of us, who live our lives according to the word of God and common sense, we should not have to foot the bill for their sins"—and then juxtaposes this view against the terrified words of a Nighttimer who could be shot for inadvertently violating the morning curfew—"You ever found yourself trapped in a world where you're everybody's worst nightmare?" (223–24). Some say that Rant died in a car accident, but others believe that he crashed his car in order to go back in time and thus is still alive. Simms argues that Rant's time-travel theories were insane, but Simms could be lying so that others will not compete with his own trips back in time to make himself stronger and richer.

The government, acting in defense of established society, considered Rant to be a threat. If he caused a rabies contagion, then he was a menace to public health. Even if he did not have rabies, his unruly behavior seemed to be spreading, inspiring the Nighttimers to defy the social order. The demolition derbies or "Party Crashing" that Rant encouraged, which brought Nighttimers together in the illegal act of destroying cars, could have grown into an organized resistance to the status quo, a breaking of the morning curfew and a claim to the same human rights as the Daytimers. As one Nighttimer muses, "Weren't we the revolution that every night almost happened . . . but instead we just crashed into each other? If just one leader would emerge—Rant Casey or anybody—the army of us, ready to fight and die, wouldn't we be invincible?" (228). But Rant's apparent death in a car crash seems to have scared Nighttimers away from participating in acts like his with the potential for social revolution, and now only Daytimer kids are the ones imitating him, pretending to drool as if they had rabies and acting out in teenage rebellion against their middle-class parents.

Whether idealizing or demonizing him, each side projects its own view onto Rant, freezing him into a static myth: "The government says Rant's alive because they need a villain. The kids say Rant's alive because they need a hero" (297). But Rant—the angel face with the monster snot, the sensitive lover with the infectious animal drool, the dead car-crash victim who may yet be alive—remains a cipher, apparently undefined by others and undetermined by the past. In his depiction of the human/animal, living/dead Rant, Palahniuk was inspired by philosopher Jacques Derrida's notion of the "zombie" as "something that isn't human anymore but has the appearance of a human. Something that is more animal than human being." Palahniuk shares Derrida's fascination with the zombie in that "it is so unresolved—it is not alive and it is not dead, and it's not an animal [or a human]."[14]

Society feels threatened by that which does not fit its categories. According to Palahniuk, when Rant "has slipped too far into that animal identity," he "must be destroyed"[15]—that is to say, the government *decides* that Rant has become a rabid animal to be eliminated, to be rendered dead. But the novel does not resolve Rant's situation in the end. It does not foreclose on the possibility that Rant is still out there somewhere in the present, his senses alive with an animal awareness of others' suffering, his body capable of refusing to act in the ways expected of him by the powers that be. If there is still the chance that Rant can defy Simms and save his mother, then there is hope for us all.

Pygmy

Like Rant, Pygmy must constantly contend with others' attempts to define him. The leaders of his homeland, some unnamed fascist/totalitarian state, kidnap him from his parents at age four and subject him to ideological indoctrination. Told that their parents were killed by an American terrorist bomb, Pygmy and other children are brainwashed into becoming agents in a secret revenge plot against the United States. They are to infiltrate small-town America in the guise of foreign-exchange students, with the ultimate mission of spreading a deadly neurotoxin across the country. Once he is lodged with his host family in a midwestern U.S. town, thirteen-year-old Pygmy is barraged with jingoistic rhetoric from the other side. Having been taught to revere his "glorious homeland" in its righteous fight against the "Venomous vipers of capitalist imperial United States," Pygmy now finds that the Americans consider theirs to be "the greatest country on earth" and that they denigrate him as a "coarse, uneducated, illiterate boy" who is the product of a "savage dictatorship reluctant to admit the faintest light of free speech or Christian charity."[16] Despite his sense of his own dignity, strength, and intelligence, he is called a "dirty, sickly orphan" and a "puny, ignorant child" (122), or, in the even blunter words of his host brother, a "little turd" (4) and a "'tard" (5). The very name "Pygmy" is a racist diminutive imposed upon him by those who cannot be bothered to learn his real name, let alone his true character.

As with Rant, Palahniuk conceived of Pygmy as "kind of a cypher": "This allows everyone who meets Pygmy and interacts with him to project their worst prejudices, self-righteousness and bigotry onto him. They're not even sure what race he is. His name isn't even really Pygmy."[17] The idea for this character first came to Palahniuk when he was volunteering at a homeless soup kitchen and the people there began to make up stories about him as a sex offender, an arsonist, or a murderer now forced to do community service: "all these horrific things had been projected on me because no one knew what to make of this white guy who showed up and made toast at 5 o'clock every morning."[18] Writing in the voice of Pygmy, who narrates the novel, Palahniuk can perhaps help readers of all races, even Caucasians like himself, to imagine what it might feel like to be the victim of others' prejudiced projections.

One reason Pygmy is viewed as uneducated and illiterate is that American customs and the English language are foreign to him. When a local pastor baptizes another teenage secret agent, Magda, so that she can "die" and be reborn in Christ, she and Pygmy, unfamiliar with the ritual, take the verbal reference to death literally and fear that she is being drowned as a human sacrifice.

Later, when Pygmy approaches an American middle-school girl at a dance, his greeting—"Respected potential reproductive vessel, request engage preliminary foreplay ritual prior genital coitus"—earns the response, "Shove off, freak" (57–58). Palahniuk had a similar experience with miscommunication when, on a European book tour, he attempted to speak German and inadvertently "said stuff like, 'It's amazing how many Germans have been inside me.'"[19] On another occasion, while trying to say, "*Es tut mir leid dass ich so viel Deutsch vergessen habe*" ("I'm sorry that I've forgotten so much German"), he actually said, "*Es tut mir leid dass ich so viele Deutsche vergast habe*" ("I'm sorry that I gassed so many Germans").[20] Everyone is a "foreigner" somewhere; no one's speech is immune to misunderstanding. Palahniuk is well aware that his own ancestors struggled with English, and he has said that Pygmy's pidgin language is in part "based on my oldest Ukrainian immigrant relatives, who spoke in a kind of broken way."[21] In an even more personal connection with Pygmy, Palahniuk has spoken frankly about his own linguistic difficulties as a child, noting that, even though he was born in America, "I was the last kid in my class who learned how to read and write"[22] and that "English is like my second language."[23]

Pygmy is a novel about language use and its consequences, the ways in which words affect our view of ourselves and the world. When Pygmy and his host brother visit a local Walmart, a boy named Trevor calls Pygmy a "little colored bitch" and tells the brother to "go fuck" him (12). Then, when Trevor shouts racist taunts at Pygmy about his lack of masculinity—"You come from one of those dick-mutilation places?" (16)—Pygmy forcibly sodomizes him in the store restroom. The words that go through Pygmy's mind during the act reveal his understanding of the situation and why he commits the rape. He thinks of his sex organ as a "stabbing" "weapon," which he deploys while also "flogging" Trevor by repeatedly calling *him* a "bitch" (18). Pygmy thinks of Trevor's blue anus leaking red blood onto the white wall as linked to the American flag, which is going down in defeat. Pygmy's act is thus shaped by the words and ideas in which he has been indoctrinated, by his belief that his homeland suffered a terrorist attack from America and that he must strike back in order to restore his country's pride and strength. Trevor becomes a symbol of U.S. imperialism, and Pygmy is the agent by which his country retaliates.

But are Pygmy's actions entirely dictated by homeland doctrine? It is curious that he takes some of the money that Trevor stole from the host brother and returns it to him. Why would Pygmy care about his *American* brother? Pygmy may want to ingratiate himself with his host family, but it could also be that he is beginning to move beyond his ideological conditioning and to feel some sympathy for the "enemy." The host brother was bullied, too, and Pygmy had witnessed him crying as Trevor's shoe pressed down onto his face. Pygmy's retaliation against Trevor, who is in turn held down and made to cry, may be as much on behalf of the host brother as it is in defense of the homeland. The violence Pygmy does to Trevor, which additionally includes forced oral entry, could also be seen as Palahniuk's imagined revenge for his own former self, for he too was once a victim of bullying. "When I was in high school," he has said, "the jocks used to stand in the hallways and yell, 'Palahniuk, suck my dick!' See, it rhymes. The chorus of my teen years."[24]

Some days after Trevor was assaulted, he threatens Pygmy with a gun and professes to love him. Pygmy reduces Trevor's confused feelings to a simple verbal formula, Stockholm syndrome, dismissing and denigrating them as merely a pathological condition in which the victim identifies with the aggressor. Then, when Trevor starts shooting other students in a Columbine-style massacre, Pygmy uses his martial-arts training to decapitate him. Yet, despite this violent assertion of difference, Pygmy is haunted by the sense that there may be some likeness between himself and Trevor, that relationships may be more complicated than his verbal formulas and rote training have allowed him to see. In a scene where Pygmy has camouflaged his own face for a nighttime mission—"Face skin operative me, painted black, deleted"—he thinks back on Trevor's death: "all affection and hostility—erased" (108). Not only does Pygmy seem to have some inkling that both he and Trevor have used violence to avoid facing life's complexities, he also appears to sense that, by killing Trevor, he has destroyed a part of himself.

Pygmy has been taught to believe in a cruel god and told that he should commit crimes in order to be worthy of that god's punishment. It is this teaching that he repeats to himself in order to justify his rape and decapitation of Trevor. In the process, Pygmy also protected his host brother and fellow students from Trevor's bullying and shooting, but this is a less conscious motive, since these are Americans and thus ostensibly his enemies.

Pygmy's killing of the church pastor, Reverend Tony, marks another step in his peculiar progress toward enlightenment. Pygmy enters the church with its statue of Christ, whose crying and bleeding symbolize understanding of others' sin and compassion for their suffering. For Pygmy, though, these are signs of weakness that go along with the absence of a phallus: "look under loincloth where only plaster. No weapon" (26). Pygmy has discovered that his fellow teenage agent, Magda, was impregnated by Reverend Tony. Acting cruelly to please his cruel god, Pygmy kills the reverend by lacing Magda's panties with neurotoxin and having him sniff them.

Pygmy's act could also be seen as an attempt to protect Magda and other girls from future predations; he knows that the reverend also made sexual advances to Pygmy's American host sister. But, even as he is eradicating the evil reverend whom he calls "devil Tony" (194), Pygmy is half-aware of a strange likeness between them. Just as the reverend is faced with panties that contain his semen and Magda's blood, so Pygmy still has some of the money stained with his own semen and Trevor's blood. How different is Pygmy from Reverend Tony, given that they both are rapists? What right does Pygmy have to sit in cruel, righteous judgment over "devil Tony" when he himself could be condemned for the same sin?

When Pygmy attends the church funeral for Trevor, he sees the boy's parents weeping for him. The expression he uses for their tears—"water bleeding out eyes" (148)—is the same phrase he thinks of in connection with the Christ statue. Out of growing compassion for the parents' suffering, Pygmy considers confessing his rape of Trevor and his subsequent rejection of the boy's love so that the reasons for the shooting rampage could be better understood. When Trevor's father is charged with having sexually abused his son and he and his wife cry as he is arrested, Pygmy's feeling for them almost leads him to confess that he was the one who assaulted the boy. When his host father is arrested for a theft that Pygmy himself committed and he witnesses the weeping of his host mother and his host sister, with whom he is falling in love, Pygmy is increasingly torn between the sympathy he feels for his American family and the cruelty he is expected to show to the "enemy." Although Pygmy resists being indoctrinated into Christianity—"Statue man still dead, plaster bleeding red paint" (205)—the blood and tears of others' suffering affect him. He is feeling his way toward his own beliefs, in defiance of the "cruel deity" dogma he was taught. As the weeping host mother presses Pygmy to her breast, her tears fall onto his hair and leave their imprints on his "Property of Jesus" T-shirt (229), as if he himself were crying. It is as though Pygmy is having physically impressed upon him the need for Christ-like compassion, moving him toward a bodily sympathy quite apart from religious doctrine.

The changes in Pygmy's attitude toward his family can be gauged from the way his personal feelings begin to affect the rote phrases he normally uses. One early view of his relationship with his host sister involves the metaphor of rape as conquest of a foreign country: "Ready weapon operative me before helpless no-clothed vagina . . . so implant seed" (170). However, as Pygmy begins to care about the girl, his language, while still aggressive and narcissistic, moves subtly toward more tenderness and generosity. After she compliments him on his eyes, he still thinks of sex as a "conquest," but he also imagines that it might "gift [her] with fetus bearing same pretty eyes as operative me" (140). When Pygmy charges that American citizen[s are] all enslaved desiring affection" (170), he is projecting onto others his own fear of how much he wants his host sister to like him. When he pleads pitifully that she not leave him behind—"This agent projecting voice beg mercy . . . Brimming eye similar baby puppy" (140–41)—he tries to convince himself that he is merely putting on a pretense of caring for the sake of his mission, but he is also mocking himself for sentimental feelings and struggling with real fears of abandonment.

Similarly, Pygmy's false smiles of affection for his host mother—"Fashion face of operative me passable facsimile expression of caring" (166)—gradually grow into true concern, as if the physical act of faking emotion had countered the very idea of pretense, challenging the dogma of hatred for foreigners and replacing it with an enacted love. When Pygmy runs to kiss his tearful mother and he thinks of his "Pursed lips making gesture meaning affection" (229), his pursed lips really do mean affection. The physical act, initially only pretended, has become an emotional reality. Though Pygmy's strangely impersonal and overemphatic speech continues to reveal remnants of past pretense and ideological brainwashing, he has begun to recognize his own feelings and to act on them rather than follow his homeland's dictates.

He calls his host sister "Affectionate comrade" (234), using an old term for political allegiance in a new way to show his growing commitment to her love. When he decides to sabotage the mission to spread the neurotoxin in order to save his host sister, his words show that he is following his heart rather than his head: "Body muscle operative me committing full treason. Betray own thinking machine this agent" (235). Out of sympathy for *American* suffering, Pygmy confesses that he committed the theft for which his host father was arrested, and the rape for which Trevor's father was arrested, and these two men are released from prison. Throwing himself upon the mercy of his former enemy, he seeks political asylum, along with formal adoption by his host family.

Palahniuk has described this novel as a "coming-of-age book" in which the thirteen-year-old Pygmy transitions from obedient child to rebellious teenager, then finally achieves adulthood. Pygmy in his simple-minded adherence to homeland doctrine is like a child: "For a long time, we really revere our parents. We want to do things that make them happy. We think they are faultless, the best people in the world."[25] Pygmy in his loathing and disdain for America is the rebellious teenager: "you got older and you went through this hideous age when suddenly [your parents] were the devil, they were bullies, and they didn't know anything. . . . Pygmy is trained to treat America as that bully, the oppressor, the evil idiot." Finally, Pygmy achieves a more mature perspective on others as being neither gods nor devils, neither sages nor idiots: "Eventually beyond both of these stages you break into accepting your parents as human beings who are not perfect but who love you and are really doing the very best they can. Pygmy breaks through to recognizing these evil bullies as being loving people who don't know everything."[26] By the end of the book, Pygmy has "become an adult. He finally develops empathy."[27]

Pygmy's language in the conclusion provides evidence of this growth. When he describes himself as having been "seduced by affection for American parasites" (240), he is using words in a way that challenges their received meanings. "American parasites" is negative, as if in line with the dictates of his homeland, but "affection" is positive, showing Pygmy's appreciation for his host family. "Seduced" is ambivalent, halfway between fearing and liking the fact that he has been overcome by his hosts' sweetly subtle yet overpowering influence. Pygmy's calling Americans "parasites" may betray the vestiges of his former anti-U.S. brainwashing, but he might also have decided, based on his own experiences, that a number of Americans do behave like parasites. This is a charge he levels against the journalistic media when he witnesses them acting like predators feeding off the misery of those who have suffered misfortune. No longer merely taking the meaning of words or the world as given, Pygmy is beginning to introduce complexity into his language as a sign that he is starting to view people from his own perspective.

In addition, rather than merely believing in or rebelling against others' stereotypes of him, he is beginning to verbalize his own sense of self. The last words of the novel could be considered Pygmy's first. Resigning from his role as a secret agent and sending his final dispatch to the homeland, Pygmy writes, "Begins here new life of operative me" (241). The concluding word "me" emphasizes Pygmy's newly acquired individuality. After this, the blank space on the page is the open future he can use to define himself.

CHAPTER 5

Porn Bodies and Romantic Myths

Snuff, Tell-All, Beautiful You

With the exception of two female-focused texts, *Invisible Monsters* and *Diary,* Palahniuk began his career with a series of novels centered on male protagonists: *Fight Club, Survivor, Choke,* and *Lullaby.* However, the hero of *Rant* is followed by the heroines, Cassie and Sheila, of *Snuff,* and the male focus of *Pygmy* is succeeded by the female leads, Katherine and Hazie, of *Tell-All.* On book tours, Palahniuk is one of very few authors to make a point of alternating between men and women when responding to questions from the audience. *Snuff* and *Tell-All* thus mark a turn in Palahniuk's career toward telling more female narratives, which would be borne out in the novels to come: *Damned, Invisible Monsters Remix, Doomed,* and *Beautiful You.*

I have grouped *Snuff, Tell-All,* and *Beautiful You* together because all three novels concern women trying to establish their own identities within a world that tends to reduce them to flesh or fantasy. In *Snuff,* Cassie's aspirations are cut short when she is coerced into becoming a porn performer. While Cassie is reduced to a mere body, Katherine in *Tell-All* is idealized into a mythic figure and denied the ordinary pleasures of earthly existence, including physical fulfillment. Finally, Penny in *Beautiful You* strives to find some golden mean between the unhappy extremes of porn and myth, flesh and fantasy.

Snuff

Cassie Wright is a porn star planning to set a world record by taking on six hundred men in a gangbang movie. The fictional movie is based on *The World's Biggest Gang Bang,* an actual porn film, the making of which is explored in the documentary *Sex: The Annabel Chong Story.* Palahniuk filters Cassie's story through four narrators. One is her personal assistant, Sheila, who assigns the men numbers and calls them, three at a time, when it is their turn to leave the green room and climb the stairs to join Cassie in the staged bedroom where filming occurs. The other narrators are among the waiting men: Mr. 600, Branch Bacardi, a porn veteran who first got Cassie started in the business; Mr. 137, Dan Banyan, a former TV star who hopes that his virile performance with Cassie will revive his career; and Mr. 72, Darin Johnson, a virgin who believes that Cassie is his mother. Like the multiple perspectives on Rant in the novel of that title, the different points of view on Cassie make her "sort of a screen that people project onto," as Palahniuk has explained, adding that this is true not just for "porn" performers, but for actors in "all movies": people "want these archetypes to be physical ideals that they can project their own desires and expectations on."[1]

Branch fell in love with Cassie when they were young, but she declined his offer of marriage, prioritizing her plans to have a career as a serious actress. Branch then drugged and raped her. During the act, which he filmed, Cassie died for a time, but Branch's intercourse with her restarted her heart: "Humping her dead body around that mattress, I ended the old life she had, wanting to act, and gave her a new life. Sex reincarnated that good, pure girl, but as something else."[2] Branch's imposition of his own desires onto Cassie is here represented as a kind of murder. *Her* wishes are killed, replaced with a coerced compliance on her part to *his,* as when the drugged Cassie is described as being "Slack as a blow-up sex-doll version of herself" (185). Transformed into a porn performer, she is remade into what men like Branch want, pliable to their will, regardless of what she herself wanted to be.

Cassie's past is based on that of real-life *Deep Throat* star Linda Lovelace—real name Linda Boreman—who recounts the abuse she suffered at the hands of her husband/manager in her book *Ordeal*. In fact, "Cassie Wright" is a porn pseudonym; we never learn her real name. Palahniuk got the idea for this name from Stephen King's *Carrie,* where the school principal, ignoring the protagonist's real name—Carrie White—keeps calling her Cassie Wright. In a similar way, Branch disregards his unwilling costar's real person and gives her the porn name instead.

By filming himself in the act of compelling her to become compliant flesh, Branch also denies whatever humane feelings he may have as a person and casts himself in the role of a rapist. Even as he turns her into an icon of passive femininity who will have "pink plastic vaginas" cast from her "shaved pussy," Branch also reduces himself to a "dick," as evidenced by the "silicone-rubber copies of his erection" that will be sold as sex toys (41). Trapped in the role of priapic playboy—Branch Bacardi is his porn name—he now has to live up to his reputation as an ever-ready hard body even as his skin sags and his virility flags due to aging. At times, Branch seems to realize that his career as a porn star has "arrested" his development, locking him into a "pubescent mind-set" of endless exercise to stay hard and "ejaculating on cue" to prove his virility (55). "I threw away my whole precious life, trashed my life like it was nothing but a money shot," he says at one point (109), recognizing that sex for pay has led to waste, whereas love with feeling could have meant fulfillment. If Branch had not pumped up his reputation for so long as the "biggest woodsman in porn" (65), he would be less embarrassed to admit his need for Viagra or the possibility that he has always been sterile, having "shot nothing but blanks" (64–65). But the gun metaphor here turns out to be a sign of how monstrous Branch has become under the influence of the porn industry. Even though he knows that "no human body . . . can take a pounding from six hundred hard-ons" (29), Branch intends to be Mr. 600 and, like a gunslinger notching a bullet with his kills, to write on the dildo molded from his penis that his is "The Dick That Killed Cassie Wright" (54).

Like Branch, Dan—Mr. 137—uses Cassie as a screen on which to project aspects of his own psyche. All that the men in the waiting room can see of Cassie's bedroom is the blinding white from the camera lights revealed when the door is opened to admit the next three participants in the gangbang. As these "dudes melt and disappear into the bright white" (76), Cassie starts to seem like an angel of death, taking them to sexual heaven but at the cost of their lives. Thus Cassie is simultaneously worshipped as a sex goddess on a pedestal and dreaded as the men's mortal end. Palahniuk has spoken of "everyone numbered but not knowing when their number would be called by Death—the woman at the top of the stairs in all the bright lights. A bit like in the movie *All That Jazz*—Barbara Hershey was Death, the beautiful woman dressed in white on the bed."[3] At the same time, the fact that no man is ever seen again after his time with Cassie—that is, each exits by a back door rather than returning to the green room—prompts more primal fears of her as a predator, killing each male after intercourse, as if this were "some mass black-widow-spider snuff movie" (116). Is Cassie like Messalina, the Roman empress who reputedly had men "executed" if they did not "put out" for her? (94).

Obviously, these views of Cassie as a monster have more to do with the men's "performance anxiety" (94) than with any objective sense of who she really is. Dan used to be the star of a TV detective series, but when footage surfaced of his role as the bottom in an all-male gangbang film, his career declined. The famous private dick known for "banging" every "babe" appearing on his TV show (64) now has to prove to a homophobic public that he is not gay. To advertise his attractiveness, Dan carries around a stuffed dog, a kind of literal autograph hound, on which female stars have written such testimonials as "What girl could ever say 'No' to you?!" (113). However, not only has Dan pathetically faked all these autographs, having inked this praise himself, but the writing begins to wear off so that, to take one example, "you can't tell anymore how much Julia Roberts loves him" (135). In order to ingratiate himself with Cassie, Dan has bought shampoo from her special product line, but rather than confirming his virility, it only makes his hair fall out. Dan's performance anxiety is increased by the likelihood that he may in fact be gay. In an attempt to act the part of a straight man, he keeps popping erection pills, but the overdose begins to cause blindness in one eye. Having been the object of a gangbang himself, Dan might have some sympathy for Cassie, but instead, partly due to the pressures and prejudices of the movie/TV industry, he just wants to use her to prove he is a dominant hetero male so that the headlines will read, "Dan Banyan Comes Out on Top!" (110). Uncaring about Cassie and in denial about himself, Dan desires audience adulation to the extent of having deluded dreams about marrying her and the two of them starring in a reality show to be called "*Sex Pot and the Private Dick*" (170). Tellingly, this title reduces Cassie to being a passive receptacle for Dan's dominant thrusting—but it reduces him to his sex organ, too.

As for Darin—Mr. 72—he projects onto Cassie his need for a maternal figure, believing that she was the birth mother who gave him up for adoption. When asked whether he wants to "help" rescue Cassie from porn or to "punish" her for having abandoned him, Darin's answer—"I'm here to save her" (77)—is ambiguous, for what kind of salvation does he bring? As Darin waits for his turn to be with Cassie, the bouquet of white roses he has brought for her gradually disintegrates until there is little left but "thorns" (61), the flowers having become "twisted and dark" (78). Has Darin come to restore and defend his "mother's" purity or, his love turned to hatred during his lifelong wait, to savage her in anger? Another character comments that, "whether a woman is a concubine to fuck or a damsel to redeem, she's always just some passive object to fulfill a man's purpose" (21). When Darin was young, he tried to get close to his mother by buying some of the Cassie sex toys molded from her vagina and breasts, which he treated as "religious relics" of the "perfect mother" he prayed to have (90). However, as the boy matured, his relation to the Cassie relics became increasingly sexualized. Modeling his behavior after the men in porn videos, Darin would thrust into a blow-up sex-doll of Cassie, but the more he "pumped," the more her face "collapsed" and "caved in" until nothing was left but a "murdered outline" of her on his bed (87).

Rather than making a successful transition from affection for his mother to love for another woman, Darin comes to associate sex with an inability to gain affection as his lust for the doll causes its collapse, leaving him unfulfilled. Sex is linked to desperation, failure, and violence toward the other person, the "murdered" doll. Matters are made even worse when his adopted mom discovers him with the deflated doll, which is modeled after his supposed birth mother and which he has dressed in his adopted mom's honeymoon nightgown. The latter's shock at what she views as his violation of the incest taboo fills him with shame, rendering him impotent from that moment on.

So, when Darin's number is finally called and he enters the staged bedroom for the porn shoot, he approaches Cassie with a number of unresolved issues. At first, he kneels before her in reverence, hoping that she will acknowledge him as her son. She offers him her breast to suck, saying "Come to Momma" (164). But when she then denies him recognition, claiming that the baby she gave up for adoption was a girl and treating him as if he was just another numbered performer and nothing special, he grows enraged, thrusting violently on top of her in bed. His impotence is "cured," but only in the sense that he now uses sex as a weapon to punish a woman for what he sees as the withholding of her affection. If he is going to be treated like merely another male in a gangbang, then that is what he will become, asserting dominance over her with his sex and using the porn shoot to demonstrate his virility. As Cassie rightly notes, "This kid fucks like he's got something to prove" (167), and she has to have the stagehands pull him off her before he can "fuck her to death" (168).

The fourth narrative perspective on Cassie, that of her personal assistant Sheila, was added by Palahniuk at the insistence of women in his writers' group who felt that a female voice was needed to make the book less "claustrophobic"[4] and to open it out beyond the confines of the men in the waiting room. However, despite her extensive interactions with Cassie while preparing her for the film shoot, Sheila's perspective on the porn star, at least initially, tends to be as much an imposition of her own views as was the case for the men. It turns out that Sheila is the girl that Cassie gave up for adoption, and Sheila's view of her is colored by a "lifetime of festering anger and hatred" for having been abandoned (175). Sheila wants to be recognized by her mother, but Cassie appears to be narcissistically enraptured by her own image as a porn star. Thus, when Cassie puts on dark sunglasses, Sheila hopes that the black lenses will "reflect" her in the sense of giving her back a sense of self, an identity approved by her mother. Instead, Cassie seems only to "look at herself, reflected in the window," as if seeing herself through the eyes of adoring fans. Cassie's identity seems dependent on audience approval; it is as though she is nothing but the roles she plays as a porn star, as if there is no real Cassie there at all: "The reflections of her reflections of her reflections, between the window and her black sunglasses, all those Cassie Wrights shrinking smaller and smaller, until they disappear into infinity" (50). Thus, while Cassie "looks at her reflection in the mirror above the dressing table," preening herself as a star (151), Sheila remains unrecognized, unable to reach the real mother behind the images of a porn performer: "In [Sheila's] eyes dance tiny screens of Cassie Wright, reflected" (114).

Porn seems to have ruined Sheila's life, preempting whatever relationship her mother might have had with her. Sheila thinks that Cassie chose her adult movie career over her and feels consigned to oblivion due to Cassie's stomach displaying "No stretch marks. Nothing to show for being a mother" (68). Female performers avoid taking birth-control pills because these can make their skin break out, and males avoid wearing condoms because some viewers prefer not to see them, revealing the irresponsibility of the porn industry, which allows children to be conceived and then either has them "terminated" like an "outtake" (58–59) or, as in Sheila's case, separates them from their birth mothers so that they become the "leftover veal calves of adult entertainment" (60). Rather than being granted the dignity of a daughter, Sheila feels that she is treated like a slave to a porn queen, commanded to do Cassie's make-up or give her a bikini wax, to bring her orange juice or take away her dirty tissues. Sheila believes that, instead of exploiting her in these ways, Cassie should recognize and respect her as her long-lost daughter. For Sheila, the extent of Cassie's disregard for her daughter can be measured by the name she gave her before turning her over for adoption—"the ugliest name she could imagine," Zelda Zonk (180). In answer to what appears to be her mother's hatred, Sheila responds in kind, planning to "get revenge" (175) by having Cassie die during the gangbang. Not only would the porn queen be literally screwed to death by her profession, but Sheila would profit from the life insurance and sensational video, which would sell even better as a snuff film.

Yet what Sheila discovers is that the hatred she has projected onto Cassie is false. Without letting on that she knows, Cassie has in fact recognized her as her long-lost daughter and, out of love for her, has agreed to film the record-breaking gangbang in full knowledge that she herself will perish during it, bringing financial security to Sheila. Each man that Cassie takes on is "penance" for having given Sheila up, an act of self-sacrifice in the hope that she will be "forgiven" by her daughter (54). The film is not evidence of a porn queen's narcissism but of her self-immolation, for Cassie "wants to do it in a way where she will more likely die in the process so this will be the last such movie ever allowed," as Palahniuk has explained.[5] And if the excessive sex does not kill her, Cassie plans to take a cyanide pill. The name "Zelda Zonk," which Marilyn Monroe used to refer to the side of herself that aspired to be a serious actress and not just a sex goddess, was bestowed on Cassie's daughter not out of spite, but as a form of inspiration that her child might achieve the dignity and respect that her mother had failed to attain. Cassie thus sees Sheila as the best of herself and is willing to die for her.

Up to this point, Sheila has defined herself out of hatred for a mother who she thought hated her, so the realization of Cassie's love provokes an identity crisis in the daughter, causing her to wonder, "What do you do when your entire identity is destroyed in an instant?" (184). Sheila throws away the money she took from the men who paid her for sex with Cassie, thus abjuring financial gain from her mother's misery. Sheila breaks the stopwatch she used to time the males on top of her mother—the stopwatch which formerly substituted for the "heart" she had lost but now is trying to find again (5, 197). Then, when Branch swallows the cyanide pill and when Cassie, conjoined with him at the time, is electrocuted by the defibrillator paddles used to revive him, Sheila rushes to her mother in an effort to save her. While Branch's and Cassie's "flesh" may be "married in hate, burned together" (196), the daughter has reason to believe that her mother loves her. Sheila now refers to herself as Zelda Zonk, the name Cassie gave her in the hope that her daughter would be recognized and respected. Even if Cassie failed to achieve this goal for herself, her belief in Zelda maintains this possibility for her daughter, who, at the end of the novel, still hopes that "someone might finally look and see me" (197).

Tell-All

Palahniuk returns to consider another love/hate dynamic between two female characters in *Tell-All*. Much as *Snuff* explored the ambivalent attitude that personal assistant Sheila had regarding porn queen Cassie Wright, so the new novel traces the mixed feelings of paid companion Hazie Coogan toward Hollywood legend Katherine Kenton. The author himself has noted this "commonality," while also drawing a distinction: "in one case, it's a great actress in the carnal arts of pornography, but in this case it's a great actress in that kind of pantheon of Grace Kelly and Katharine Hepburn and something that is completely not of the body." In explaining this difference, Palahniuk notes that he wrote *Tell-All* at his mother's bedside while she was dying of cancer: "maybe the reason why this actress, Katherine Kenton, is that kind of idealized, glorious character is because my mother is gone and I'm subsequently turning her into that larger-than-life, sainted, mythological angel."[6] His narrative amplification of her life into a legend was occurring, he realized, while his mother was still alive. This realization led to the central theme of the novel, which is the complex relation between the reality of a person and the fantasy of the legend we spin around that individual: "A big part of it came from the awareness, as I was taking care of my mom, that I was already mythologizing her. I was already planning the stories I would tell about how great she was, and she wasn't dead yet."[7]

As voice coach, make-up artist, and hairdresser, as personal secretary, manager, and press agent, Hazie has helped to build Katherine's reputation as a great actress. Like a "high priestess" who is "guarding" a "shrine,"[8] Hazie considers it her duty to preserve this reputation, even when this means protecting Katherine from herself and her tendency to fall for men. In describing Katherine as "among the generation of women who feel that the most sincere form of flattery is the male erection" (15), Hazie disparages Katherine's tendency to mistake male lust for love and her dependency on men to confirm her attractiveness. Hazie constantly warns her idol against engaging in "marry-kiri"—hari-kari or suicidal weddings (21)—with men who show her nothing but "opportunistic affection," like parasites that cause disease (31). Indeed, at least some of Katherine's husbands seem to have used her star status for their own advancement—Senator Warner to win reelection, Paco to further his acting career, and Terry to pass as heterosexual. Being exploited by these men caused "crow's-feet" and "frown lines" to appear in Katherine's face, threatening to mar her image (81), until Hazie gave her the facial treatments to preserve it.

The latest threat to Katherine's greatness as a Hollywood icon is Webster Westward, a young man Hazie considers to be a "charming parasite" (96) and a "scheming gigolo" (139). Hazie tears up his calling cards and throws away his flower bouquets, but still he keeps coming after Katherine. The fear is that Webster will seduce the star into marrying him by pretending to love and adore her, only so that he can then write a scandalous memoir of her, a "bile-ography" (32) or "lie-ography" (96), from which he can profit when it is published following her death. Palahniuk got the idea for the character of Webster from talking with an editor about celebrity biographies that are almost complete, pending their final chapter: "He said that all major publishing houses have these big fat biographies sitting there, waiting for people to die. All you have to do is slap on the end and put it on the market. It's that kind of commoditization and completion of your life before you die—and this kind of imposition of a public idea of self that replaces the actual living self—that I find so frightening."[9] These "death-watch biographies of aging movie stars," whose writers are just "waiting for the subject to expire so they can get a product on the shelf before the corpse gets cold,"[10] struck Palahniuk as so ghoulish that he took this "jackal/vulture culture"[11] to its next logical step in *Tell-All* by suggesting that Webster might be an actual murderer as well as a reputation killer. Hazie claims to find drafts of a Katherine Kenton biography authored by Webster that not only "rewrite her legend for his own gain" but also give details of her demise, as if her death had already occurred. The plot of Webster's lying memoir could thus be a murder plot, with his "lurid, sordid tale" replacing her life story and her life (96).

The memoir, supposedly written by Webster, initially appears to display his worshipful regard for the star: "I ask if she—the most glorious queen of theatrical culture—would consider wedding me, a mere presumptuous mortal" (100). But by praising Katherine, Webster gets to lay claim to her glory through association with her, as when he describes their sexual union as "Our shared being pasted into becoming a single living organism" (99). Webster's adulation of her turns out to be a strategy for his own self-aggrandizement; he reports "distinctly" recalling the moment when she told him, "You have the largest, most gifted penis of any man alive" (100).

Yet, in addition to burnishing Katherine's image, Webster must also tarnish it, for hagiographies do not sell as well as accounts of fallen stars, the purported "flaws and faults" in the celebrity facade which he can reveal in order to further his own literary career (83). Thus Webster's adoring prose about Katherine as a love goddess also works to undermine her, as when he juxtaposes some of the great-lady roles she played with her less decorous behavior during sex with him: "Moaning and slobbering beneath me, here was **Eleanor of Aquitaine**. Squealing and clenching, here was **Edna St. Vincent Millay**" (114). The names are printed in boldface as if they were appearing in a gossip column or scandal sheet.

Describing Katherine's "lovely, *seasoned* vagina" (98), Webster refers to the "fragile, *soiled* petals of her fecund rose" (114). He writes that, after oral sex, she "*belched* demurely" (124). He recounts his climax as one in which the "pearlescent globules of my adoration and profound admiration" are "*spattering* Katherine's unutterably beautiful visage" (115).[12] These words seem less about adoration than spite; instead of admiring Katherine, they reveal a desire to besmirch her. Palahniuk found the inspiration for Webster's peculiar form of writing in "romance novels" and their "really flowery, euphemistic language for really carnal, brutal things. So in a way I wanted to write *Tell-All* using this really over-the-top, 'beautiful' language to talk about really base things. In this case, it's a love story about hatred; the core of the book is the hatred of one person for another."[13]

The memoir would seem to show Webster's love/hate for Katherine, but the fact is that he did not write it; Hazie did, as part of a complex effort to discredit him and preserve the star's idealized image. Although Webster has not been writing a scandalous biography of Katherine or plotting to murder her, Hazie believes that he would drag the great lady down to his lowly level. His performance as a romantic lover is inferior: "**Webster Carlton Westward III** calls up the steps, noble as **William Frawley** as **Romeo Montague**, 'Kath, my dearest . . .' Calling, 'Do you have three dollars to pay the cabdriver?'" (77). Note that Hazie compares Webster to an actor playing Romeo to Katherine's

Juliet and finds him wanting, not wooing her with poetic endearments but bathetically needing her to pay his taxi fare. Hazie's standard is the idealized one of stage and screen, a world of perfect appearances, by which any mortal man will be automatically rejected as less than impeccable. "You need only look at Webb and see how no amount of Miss Kathie's love will redeem him," Hazie decides (109).

It turns out that preserving Katherine as a screen goddess means preventing her from having any real life. For her to continue to be the "wife we dream of finding" and the "mother we wish we'd had" (58), Katherine must not marry any actual man or give birth to any real children. "I've created a model of strength to which women can aspire," Hazie believes, a "living example of their own incredible possible potential" (91). If Katherine attempts to realize any of this potential, she will inevitably fall short, for reality never lives up to the fantasy legend. This is why, in Hazie's view, it is "only through a [wedding] veil that my darling Kathie most looks like her true self," "a face whom you could wed in that moment and imagine yourself happy to live with forever" (151–52). If the marriage were actually to occur, wedded bliss would encounter real-life problems and the fantasy would be destroyed. But the effect on Katherine of being cordoned off from life by Hazie, of being forced to embody the ideal, is chilling, as Palahniuk emphasizes by using metaphors that liken stardom to a kind of living death. While Hazie applies white-powder make-up to her, Katherine "stands frozen as a statue" (119), and after an ice-cube facial treatment, her "skin now feels as frigid as the sable coat preserved in cold storage" (48). "Hers is the throne, seated in the same icy pantheon as **Greta Garbo** and **Grace Kelly**," we are told (9).

Similarly, Katherine's having to live up to the image of the perfect mother cuts her off from the warmth of caring for real children. When considering possible babies for adoption, she rejects one after another because their skin is not photogenically flawless or their color does not match the room's decor. Katherine cannot help focusing on how each baby *looks,* for without the perfect baby she cannot appear as the perfect mother, and no baby is ever perfect enough: "Each innocent, Miss Kathie holds, modeling it for the foyer mirror. Doing take after take of this same scene" (76). Palahniuk suggests that the acting awards she has received, statuettes "the size of infants" and plaques "in tiny caskets" (52), are a poor substitute for children and even constitute their mortification. That winning awards and achieving fame are no replacement for living a meaningful life may be part of what Palahniuk wanted to communicate when, on book tours for *Tell-All,* he had audiences blow up inflatable—that is, empty—Oscar statuettes in order to win a prize: a big plastic turkey.

In these ways, then, the idealization of Katherine is problematic, and furthermore it tends to be self-serving on Hazie's part. Much as Webster, in the memoir we thought was written by him, put Katherine on a pedestal in order to join her there, so Hazie helps make her a star so that she herself can bask in the reflected glory. If Webster—supposedly—wrote that he "distinctly" heard the actress praise *his* greatness (100), Hazie claims in *her* narrative that only she and Katherine share the spotlight: "the pair of us are distinct as the only two figures that remain together" while "the camera tracks, always keeping us at the very center of the shot" (102–3). The more Webster and Hazie insist on the distinctiveness of their aural and visual recollections, the more we suspect them of self-serving fabrication.

And, like Webster, who claimed part of Katherine's fame by describing himself and her as "a single living organism" (99), Hazie says that it is as if she and the star are "a single entity" (103). When they were both young, Hazie was not considered conventionally beautiful enough to be a successful actress in Hollywood and so, by coaching the prettier Katherine, she found a way to achieve fame vicariously. Hazie, in living through the other woman's fame, is as dependent on audience adulation as Katherine is. As Palahniuk specifies, it is not just that the "ugly" woman, Hazie, "watches the lovely woman," Katherine, but that "the ugly woman watches the way in which the other people watch the lovely woman" (162). By coaching Katherine to be the audience's ideal, to live her life for the spotlight, Hazie deprives her of any real life, and she simultaneously deprives herself of the same.

Finally, just as Webster's admiring descriptions of Katherine barely concealed his spite, so Hazie's praise of her is often laced with malice. These many similarities between Hazie's narrative and Webster's memoir should come as no surprise since she is eventually revealed to be the one who actually wrote the biography she falsely attributes to him in order to make him look bad. Despite all the professed admiration for the star she ostensibly idealizes and supports in every way, Hazie is seething with envy and hatred of Katherine. Locked out of the bedroom while Katherine and Webster make love, jealous Hazie feels that she has been replaced in the actress's affections by an unworthy man. This humiliation is only increased when Katherine makes Hazie don a housemaid's uniform and serve Webster coffee the way he likes it. The fact is that Hazie has long chafed at being treated more like Katherine's servant than like the collaborator and equal she believes herself to be. How is it that she performs all the manual labor needed to maintain Katherine's star image and yet must always remain just outside of the spotlight while the latter gets the glory? The idea for the Hazie-Katherine relationship came to Palahniuk when, while promoting the movie version of *Choke* at the Sundance Film Festival, he noticed that the big-name actresses were often trailed by more plain-looking “handlers”: “everything that went into making the beautiful woman beautiful was being lugged around by this dumpy woman who was always far enough away that she would never get caught in the photograph. I thought it was fascinating to have that kind of Jungian separation between the ideal perfect-seeming woman and then the other woman who had to carry the burden of that perfection.”[14]

So that Katherine can shine as the star, Hazie claims to be fine with scrubbing her pots and pans, waxing her floor, walking her dog, doing her laundry and ironing, dusting and polishing her awards, fetching her whiskey, administering her drugs, and serving as her chauffeur and bodyguard. But mixed in with Hazie’s martyric itemization of all that she does for Katherine is growing resentment at being unappreciated. A lifetime of self-sacrifice, of being nothing to Katherine’s everything, has gradually turned Hazie into a vengeful, egotistical monster. While she claims to be saving Katherine from unscrupulous men by finding ways to end all her relationships, Hazie is also acting out of jealousy and selfishness, not wanting the other woman to have a marriage or children missing from her own life—and not wanting to be left alone. The two women have a ritual whereby, as each man leaves Katherine and as her face is marred by frown lines and worry wrinkles, Hazie uses a diamond ring to etch duplicates of these facial scars into a mirror. Afterward, Hazie gives Katherine facial treatments to restore her star image to its former perfection; only the mirror retains the scars, as in *The Picture of Dorian Gray,* where the portrait aged while Dorian remained youthful and unblemished. While it may seem that Hazie rescues Katherine from failed romance, Palahniuk suggests that Hazie herself is responsible for much of the scarring pain, that by keeping the star from having any real relationships, Hazie is actually the one doing her harm. It is not so much “the world” that “kills” Katherine “a little more each year” (152) as it is Hazie herself: “I cut the furrows of sadness across her forehead” (82); “I plow the diamond . . . gouging her new wrinkles and worry lines” (159), “Me mutilating her” (27).

In the end, Hazie shoots Katherine and Webster, then stages the scene to make it look as though the two of them killed each other when the actress caught him trying to steal her Oscar trophies. That Hazie is at least partly motivated by jealousy is implied by the way she describes “shooting both the lovebirds in their bedroom.” That resentment and revenge are also involved can be gleaned when Hazie gloats over seeing Katherine’s dying eyes “register the full realization that she’s been duped” by the servant who finally triumphed over her master (174). As Hazie muses in a revealingly vengeful moment, “am I Miss **Katherine Kenton**’s maid? No more so than the butcher plays handmaiden to the tender lamb” (7).

Of course, Hazie deludes herself into thinking that her motives are pure. In Hazie's mind, the actual Katherine is the lamb that must be sacrificed in order to ensure the perpetuity of her legend as an actress. Though in reality Webster may have truly loved her and the two of them might have made a life together, such an ordinary outcome would destroy the myth of Katherine's greatness, the legend that Hazie has given *her* life to creating. And so Webster must be cast as the villain, trying to steal the star's reputation by writing a scandalous biography and purloining her awards, while Katherine must play the heroic victim in a "grand finale" that is "drenched in glory and pathos" (173). "This is what love is," Haze convinces herself, believing that by killing Katherine she has "rescued her, who she was in the past and who she will be to the future" (172). But what about the present? By orienting her existence so entirely around the spotlight, by embodying a legend for her millions of fans, Katherine never got to live for herself in the present—and neither did Hazie, since she was the "high priestess" who spent her life "guarding" Katherine's "shrine" (14).

Tell-All's ending can be usefully compared to that of *Snuff,* which takes an opposite trajectory. In *Snuff,* personal assistant and stage manager Sheila has been slaving away for porn queen Cassie Wright, plotting to kill her for her cruel disregard. However, Cassie finally grants Sheila the recognition she craves, repenting for having done her wrong. The porn star decides to end her own career in the spotlight and sacrifice herself for Sheila, whom she now acknowledges as her long-lost daughter. Responding in kind, Sheila then attempts to save Cassie's life and accepts the name her mother gave her. This name, "Zelda Zonk," which Marilyn Monroe used to signify her desire for dignity and respect, indicates that Sheila may actually fulfill Cassie's wish to live a meaningful life as something other than a sex symbol in front of the cameras. By contrast, in *Tell-All,* actress Katherine Kenton never acknowledges Hazie's contributions and unrepentantly continues to exploit her. Whereas Cassie and Sheila return to reality, Katherine and Hazie remain trapped in movie fantasy, with the actress unable to live a life apart from being a Hollywood legend because Hazie will not let her. In the end, Hazie kills the real Katherine to preserve the legend and then adopts a child called "Norma Jean Baker"—the name Marilyn Monroe had before she became a star. Palahniuk here horrifyingly suggests that Hazie will groom her adopted daughter to become another Hollywood legend like Katherine. The cycle of fame and misery will continue.

Beautiful You

To maintain the fantasy of her Hollywood legend, Katherine in *Tell-All* was kept from enjoying real life. And what about the fans who go to her movies and read books about her? Are the consumers of such mediated experiences not similarly deprived of actual existence? Palahniuk has said that, in *Beautiful You,* "I wanted to write about how many of us, when we look back at the major events in our lives, they're not actually things that happened to us. They're our favorite movie, our favorite book, things that weren't full experiences; they were facilitated by a product that we bought." Palahniuk's concern is that too many people "find an identity in a series of products, and experiences provided by those products, rather than by going out and having strong, unique experiences of their own."[15] Among these products are "chick flicks" and "chick lit," types of escapist films and fiction that now have legions of avid female fans. Palahniuk has described *Beautiful You* as "a mash-up of the most popular chick lit novels. . . . The original title was *Fifty Shades of the Twilight Cave Bear Wears Prada.*"[16]

Like Andrea Sachs, the much-abused personal assistant to a high-powered fashion editor in *The Devil Wears Prada,* Palahniuk's heroine Penny Harrigan is treated like a lowly intern at a New York law firm, constantly ordered to fetch coffee and round up extra chairs for the senior partners at meetings. Yet, like Andrea, naive Penny remains absurdly hopeful, telling herself, "The days were long here [at the firm], but they could be exciting."[17] Just as Andrea has a down-to-earth boyfriend, Alex, so Penny dates plain, hardworking Tad. Liking his "sunny, take-charge outlook on life," Penny "found that she enjoyed pulling in harness with this hopeful go-getter" (109).

But all this changes when Penny meets dotcom billionaire Cornelius Linus Maxwell, who draws her into a world of material fulfillment and sexual delight, much as wealthy powerbroker Christian Grey seduces Ana Steele in *Fifty Shades of Grey.* Christian showers Ana with lavish gifts and overwhelms her with his physical attentions: "Before I know it, he's got both of my hands in one of his in a viselike grip above my head, and he's pinning me to the wall using his hips. Holy shit. His other hand grabs my hair and yanks down, bringing my face up, and his lips are on mine. It's only just not painful. I moan into his mouth, giving his tongue an opening. He takes full advantage, his tongue exploring my mouth. I have never been kissed like this."[18] The interaction here borders on violence, and her pleasure is very close to pain. Are Christian's gifts a bribe so that he can work his sadistic will on Ana? Palahniuk's satiric take on *Fifty Shades of Grey* in *Beautiful You* makes it clear that Maxwell's sexual treatment of Penny *is* domineering—"finding ways to coerce her to greater satisfaction" (57)—and harmful: "He'd drive her to climax until her back ached and her legs wouldn't work" (59). Moreover, Palahniuk emphasizes the extent to which Maxwell's expensive gifts are lures whereby he induces her to succumb to his ultimately painful ministrations. He may buy her fancy dresses and take her to dinner at the top of the Eiffel Tower, but material possessions are no cover for his cold lack of love: "Penny felt a chill down her spine, exposed by the plunging back of her Vera Wang gown" (43); "She dreamed of plummeting from the top of the Eiffel Tower. She was falling because Maxwell had pushed her" (56).

But Penny ignores her premonitory dreams, preferring instead to remain in a "chick lit" fantasy of material comfort and celebrity acclaim. Set up in a swanky apartment paid for by Maxwell, Penny "snuggled under the smooth sheets, naked, nibbling on a brioche, sipping a latte" (90). As consort to a rich and powerful man, she basks in the fame, spotting references to herself in the *New York Post* headlines—"Nerd Prince Plucks New Cinderella" (36)—and seeing her name "in boldface among the other celebrity names on Page Six" (21), like Hollywood star Katherine Kenton in *Tell-All*. But the reality underlying this fantasy is increasingly dire. Maxwell has been using her body to perfect a line of sex toys, which he has sold to millions of females lured by the prospect of erotic fulfillment. These toys have hatched inside them, introducing nanobots that have traveled to the women's brains and that now induce pleasurable sensations whenever they buy Maxwell's products. Penny sees her girlfriend Monique along with other zombie hordes of women, their minds enslaved to bodily impulses controlled by Maxwell, forcing them all to buy his corporation's products: the same sex toys, "the same ugly, clunky shoes," and "the same vampire romance novel" (123), probably Stephenie Meyer's *Twilight,* the original inspiration for *Fifty Shades of Grey*. Monique then barricades herself in her room, "slavishly diddling herself" into a near-coma with Maxwell's sex toys and causing Penny great concern (169), much as Andrea worries when her roommate Lily slips into a comatose state in *The Devil Wears Prada*.

When Penny threatens to expose Maxwell's evil empire, he uses his remote control to trigger the nanobots inside her to overwhelm her body with unwanted stimuli: "Helpless, Penny felt her body respond to an invisible attacker. Her orifices ached as if she were being violated by hundreds of erect penises" (201). Palahniuk makes it clear that this is not some romantic ravishment; "This was some savage satellite-relayed rape" (161). To counteract this phallic assault, Penny journeys to a cave in the Himalayan mountains to learn about primal female powers from an ancient sex-witch known as Baba Gray-Beard—a nod to Jean M. Auel's *The Clan of the Cave Bear*. Returning to the city, Penny then does battle with the evil entrepreneur, deflecting one of Maxwell's own rocketing dildos back at him, which results in his death by castration. Penny and the millions of women he enslaved are thereby freed.

The idea for *Beautiful You* came to Palahniuk when he remembered himself as a child discovering some porn paperbacks hidden in his father's closet.

These fictions, featuring titles "like *Girl on Girl Ranch Studs* and *Gestapo Pussy Ranch*"[19] and containing descriptions of "graphic, mechanistic sex,"[20] seemed written in some alien code that made no sense to him. But his mother's romance novels were equally indecipherable to the boy, who found them "so flowery and so euphemistic" that it was hard to tell when something "carnal" was supposed to be happening.[21] Did a sentence such as "He plunged the full length of his steely manhood . . . into her salty chambers" mean that "he just stabbed her in the ear"?[22] Recalling these early "literary" discoveries got Palahniuk thinking about gendered reading habits. Male pornographic fictions and female euphemistic romances seemed to be opposite extremes, the former brutally physical—as if "written by really clunky machines"[23]—and the latter so "soft focus" and emotional that there sometimes appeared to be no sexual bodies in them at all. To show up this disparity, Palahniuk decided that he would juxtapose the two extremes, putting the pornographic right up against the romantic in what he calls "gonzo-erotica": "What if you could write a kind of Marquis de Sade pornography, really brutal stuff, but in the euphemisms of Barbara Cartland?"[24]

Consider the way in which Palahniuk writes about the interaction between Maxwell and Penny. She sees him in idealistic terms. During their Paris rendezvous, the "warm wind tousled his blond hair" (45) and he uncorks a bottle of pink champagne. However, he then proceeds to use a "vaginal syringe" to douse her sex with the liquid (47), which turns out to be a "pink-champagne douche" that he is product testing (133). In phrases like "champagne douche product" (82), the romance of champagne runs up against the reality of the body and its crass commercialization; the fantasy of pink is made flesh. Again and again, Palahniuk juxtaposes Penny's sentimental dreams and Maxwell's blunt physicality (emphasis added): "Between marathon sessions of arousal culminating in mind-shattering orgasms, Maxwell *lectured Penny. He slipped a wet finger into her, matter-of-factly saying, 'This is your urethra'*" (53). In a "voice muted with admiration and wonder," he tells her, "This is exceptional. *Do you always ejaculate this much?*" (54). He promises her that "you'll experience more satisfaction than you ever dreamed possible" in the moment when "*I release the pressure*" and "*the blood will rush to your uris major*" (51). Palahniuk's "gonzo-erotica" exaggerates gender differences to show how polarized the two sexes are, as revealed in the divergent words they use to understand their relationship. When Maxwell says that he has "dissected many cadavers, both male and female, to understand the mechanics of pleasure" (46), his focus on mere physicality seems to deprive the body of any animating spirit. For her part, Penny "wanted to believe that making love was more than just fiddling with nerve endings until harum-scarum chemicals squirted around limbic systems." However, her notion of the ideal relationship is so ethereal and sentimental that it seems to lack any grounding in physical reality: "Real love, she knew, was something lasting and soulful. It sustained and nourished a person" (73).

Despite their differences, porn and romances are both escapist fictions, reducing complex characters to caricatures and simplifying life's uncertainties into predictable formulas, whether these be raunchy ("*Girl on Girl Ranch Studs*")[25] or romantic ("something lasting and soulful"). As Palahniuk has noted, "porn always ends the same way. It's the same reason why [my mother and] my grandma went through a hundred Harlequin romances a year."[26] "Porn is the adult version of the fairytale," he added. "There's a real comforting sameness to it. It's never going to end badly."[27] And yet the very certainty of these fictions' happy ending is what makes them so dangerously addictive, because it is so much easier to read about a sentimental spirit or a willing body than it is to encounter real people with an unpredictable combination of body and soul.

Perhaps it is the seductive way in which such formulaic fictions replace reality, seeming to trigger knee-jerk responses in their readers—swooning or climaxing—that led Palahniuk to link these fictions to teledildonics, sex toys activated by remote control to pleasure a person's body. Ever the satirist, Palahniuk takes the popular novels that people so readily consume to be romanced or titillated and then projects a future in which happy "sex" can occur without any potentially troublesome face-to-face or skin-to-skin contact. Teledildonics is, as he says, "just an extension of how much of our lives are not genuine experiences; they're these commodified, purchased, downloaded, pirated, secondhand experiences that are crafted for us. We're not allowed to go out and have our own adventures or make our own mistakes because there's just so many things readily consumable for us."[28] As the technology blog Gizmodo notes, a number of companies are in fact marketing "social sex toys" that "let long-distance partners 'feel' each other in real-time via data-enabled devices." As one example, "there's OPue, a vibrating dildo equipped with sensors that remotely stimulate."[29]

As Penny finds out, sex toys not only addict their users to facile pleasures, they also enslave their consumers to corporate masters like Maxwell—a subjugation made even worse by teledildonics. Palahniuk links such cybersex technology, which provides a "commodified experience that replaces a moment of intimacy," to "rape": "you could extend that commodified experience to the point where, if you allow someone else, if you do delegate your pleasure to a machine or to a group of scientists that create the machine, then you're in danger of being subject to them,"[30] as Penny is assaulted by Maxwell's remotely triggered stimuli. It is clear that Palahniuk's satire of romance fiction, porn novels, and teledildonics is designed to warn us away from "these faux-yet-intense substitutes for human relationships"[31] and to lead us back to risky but real encounters, ones where failure is as much a possibility as fulfillment. Porn and romances may lead inevitably to a happy ending, but since they offer only ersatz experiences—climaxes without love, swooning without sex—they are ultimately unsatisfying. Real relationships may also lack love or sex, but they represent the only possibility of combining the two for true fulfillment.

There are some potentially hopeful signs near the end of *Beautiful You.* Although Maxwell had "taught her about pleasure without love," Penny learns from her wise mentor Baba Gray-Beard that "profound ecstasy could coexist with an even stronger affection" (170). Even Maxwell turns out to have wanted more than sexual domination. Granted, he exploits women's pleasure to control their buying habits, but Penny's additional fear that he used the sex toys to implant embryonic clones of himself in millions of women proves unfounded. Instead of desiring to replicate his own power, he implanted only one embryo, that of his deceased wife, in the hope that he could thereby be "reunited with his beloved" (215). Brutally physical Maxwell thus turns out to harbor a hidden wish for everlasting love.

The carnal yet ultimately romantic Maxwell is "old enough to be [Penny's] father" (47). Ancient Baba Gray-Beard, the randy sex-witch who teaches Penny about affection, becomes a kind of mother to her. Palahniuk has described *Beautiful You* as an attempt to "resolve the [graphic, mechanistic] kind of pornography that my father read and the [romantic, euphemistic] kind of pornography that my mother read,"[32] to "wed them together."[33] Could it be that the ultimate goal of his "gonzo-erotica" is not to juxtapose male porn and female romance in order to show the extreme disparity between them, but rather to bring them together, as he has often spoken of wishing that he could have reunited his father and his mother after their divorce?[34]

An understanding of this as Palahniuk's goal—to reconcile male and female, flesh and fantasy—may help to explain some equivocal aspects of the novel's ending. After freeing women from Maxwell's teledildonic control, his reduction of them to mere bodies in heat, Penny follows Baba Gray-Beard's example, abjuring phallic technology and planning instead to teach women to make love to their bodies with "safe rudimentary personal care tools from the raw materials provided by nature" (182), since "Love was paramount" (217). However, Penny finds that she misses the "high-tech vaginal stimulation" of Maxwell's teledildonics (217), and so she begins to use his remote control to activate the pleasure centers of her own and other women's brains so that they can all achieve climax—an ecstasy that may feel real but is in fact "only a nanobot-induced hallucination" (221).

What are we to make of this ending? Does it matter that, unlike Maxwell who was selfish and domineering, Penny is attempting to use her power in a "generous" way and for the women's own good (221), helping them to "celebrate their bodies with vigorous self-romancing" (220)? Even a "benevolent lady dictator" is still a dictator; women whom Penny would "pummel with joy" (221) and "carpet-bomb with self-esteem" (222) are still being attacked. Moreover, what if Penny has merely succumbed to arousal addiction, the need for more and more "Artificial overstimulation" (131) promoted by male technology, which has perverted mother nature? Penny cannot help hearing Baba Gray-Beard's voice in her head, warning her to destroy the "evil controller device . . . before it *seduces*" her just as Maxwell did (219). It is possible to read Penny as entirely self-deluded, believing that she is spreading love when really she is assaulting women, thinking that she is upholding Baba Gray-Beard's values when in fact she has been seduced by Maxwell's ways.

But in the end Penny refuses to choose between paternal and maternal influences. Rather, she strives to reconcile flesh and fantasy—which the novel has presented as the two extremes of modern male technology and ancient female wisdom. On the book's last two pages, Penny is enjoying a deep communion with Baba Gray-Beard, remembering with pleasure all that the old mystic has taught her about love and female fulfillment. But then Penny finds herself thinking, "Perfect as this moment was . . . even this scene could be improved upon." Picking up Maxwell's controller device, she uses it teledildonically to hallucinate a vision of a naked Ron Howard as a "robust, strapping figure" who "swaggered boldly toward her" (221–22). As much as Penny feels the appeal of mother nature, she cannot give up on the idea of technological improvements. But, unlike Maxwell, Penny uses the remote control to trigger more than just porn sensations; it also conjures up the romantic vision of a handsome lover. Now that Penny is the one in control, she attempts to deploy technology in the service of her own desires, creating something new that combines flesh and fantasy. The actor Ron Howard, who played Opie on *The Andy Griffith Show* and Richie on *Happy Days,* is known for his boyish innocence and his sweet sensitivity; he is about as far from manly swagger as one can get. But what if he could be both boldly sexual and sensitive to her needs? This is what Penny creatively imagines when she extends the actor's endowment beyond his cutely boyish complexion to envision "His impressive, freckled-pink manhood [which] swung heavily between his legs" (222). Penny's gonzo-erotica is a hilarious mash-up of porn and romance, flesh and feeling. But, beyond the hilarity, there is still the hope that sex and sentiment—too often viewed as opposites—can be brought together. "I like to reinvent the language around sex," Palahniuk has said, "because writing a sex scene is boring and mundane [as in a clichéd romance], or boring and graphic [as in formulaic porn]. But if you reinvent the language of it, you can reinvent the act itself."[35]

CHAPTER 6

Palahniuk's Divine Comedy

Damned, Doomed

We have seen how Penny in *Beautiful You* hopes to bring some romantic sensibility and uplift to base pornographic content. Palahniuk experiments with another disparity between style and subject matter in *Damned,* where a thirteen-year-old girl named Madison suddenly finds herself in hell. Of course, this is not the first time that Palahniuk has filtered serious, even tragic, topics through a young teen's perspective. Other thirteen-year-olds who have faced dire circumstances include Pygmy (terrorist indoctrination), Rant (tragic lineage), and the boys in "Guts" (sexual shame and worse). In writing these works, Palahniuk drew inspiration from classic American literature such as *Huckleberry Finn* and *Tom Sawyer,* books he described as "vehicles by which the reader could explore much, much darker issues like slavery, like the industrialization of America, through this very innocent perspective," that of "an uneducated child."[1] Now Madison, who identifies herself as a "proactive thirteen-year-old chubby girl,"[2] becomes the eyes through which we explore such solemn matters as sin and suffering, as she guides us through a hell filled with damned souls.

In fact, this is the first in "a series of three books in which Madison visits hell, purgatory and eventually heaven," according to Palahniuk, who describes his trilogy as "very much an homage to Dante."[3] Palahniuk has modeled *Damned, Doomed,* and *Delivered* on the *Inferno,* the *Purgatorio,* and the *Paradiso,* the three parts of Dante's *Divine Comedy,* a fourteenth-century religious epic poem. Palahniuk's books even have faux red-leather binding and gilt lettering on the spine, aping the great literary classics. But where Dante's epic is doctrinaire in content and serious in tone—the *Divine Comedy* in its title refers only to the fact that it ends happily in Paradise—the snarky teen narrator of Palahniuk's mock epic is not inclined to accept preconceived ideas about sin, damnation, or anything else, which tends to make her journey through hell a much funnier experience.

Damned

Madison's hell is different from Dante's Inferno, to the point where she accuses the poet of having "hoisted a generous helping of campy make-believe on the reading public" (8). Of course, Palahniuk is well aware that many would consider his own version of the nether regions to be just such "campy make-believe." Dante's narrator is the horrified witness of damned souls suffering fiery torment. Madison, with the irrepressible optimism of youth, tends to take a rosier view of the proceedings, such as when she notes that the flames, steam, and smoke "combine to create a perpetual rustic après-ski atmosphere" (22). For her, "Hell isn't so dreadful . . . especially not compared to junior high school" and "having your legs waxed or getting your navel piercing done at a mall kiosk. Or bulimia" (20). Yes, Madison is a spoiled little rich girl whose opinions can be viewed as childish ignorance of the true severity of adult torment. But her words can also be read as calling attention to the fact that adults—such as the ones in hell—do not have a monopoly on pain; the lives of teens can involve real suffering. Regarding bulimia, Madison remarks that not so long ago "girls with eating disorders" would be subjected to exorcisms in order to "evict the occupying demon" that was thought to be possessing them (41). In this way, Madison points out that what was once interpreted as a religious matter of good and evil is now considered to be a medical condition of wellness or ill health. *Pace* Dante, perhaps not everything is a potential sin.

Each denizen of Dante's Inferno has been consigned to his or her proper circle of hell, doomed to suffer according to their particular sin. Though Dante may feel sympathy for some of them, for him there is no question that they have all been justifiably condemned. Madison is not so sure. While reasons may perhaps be found for why "98.3 percent of lawyers end up in Hell," should "100 percent of journalists and redheads" be sent there too? (108). Given his journalistic background, Palahniuk himself might have cause to complain, and singling out redheads seems prejudiced or arbitrary. When Madison is then told that "100 percent of people who die of AIDS are consigned to Hell" (126), she has a right to wonder about the justice of the value system that is being enforced. As part of a "salvation polygraph test" (197), Madison is asked whether she views "sexual acts between individuals of the same gender to be an abomination" (93). Dante accepts the doctrinaire view that "sodomites" belong in hell, but Madison wonders instead about the kind of deity that could promote such bigotry: "Is God . . . homophobic . . . ? Or is God testing to see if I am?" (93). It appears that Madison is also expected to disapprove of interracial marriage and to applaud the fact that "horny angels" who mated with "mortal women" were "cast into Hell to become demons" (80). But she rebels, denouncing such attitudes as "racist" (94) and hypocritical, given God's own assignation with the Virgin Mary in the form of the Holy Spirit: "it would seem that the only immortal being allowed to indulge in a dalliance with mortals is God Himself" (81).

In Dante's Inferno, demons are loathsome creatures to be abhorred, but Madison and her other teenage friends in Palahniuk's hell have a sneaking admiration for the demons they encounter. Bad boy Archer "flashes a thumbs-up" at a demon for eating a lawyer (81). Nerdy Leonard calls another demon "pretty rad" after the fiend dismembers and devours football jock Patterson (28). Here the demons are applauded not so much for doing God's work as for rebelling against the status quo, enacting the kind of insurrection that disaffected teenagers dream of. It is in this same spirit that Madison compliments a demon by saying that she "loved the scene [in *The Exorcist*] where he made the little girl, Regan, crab-walk backward down the stairs with gore spilling out of her mouth" (91). Beyond the humor of Madison's childish ignorance—mistaking a movie for real life, seeing special effects rather than suffering—there is a more serious point about rebellion: like Regan, Madison has been a sweet and submissive girl, a real Miss Goody Two-Shoes, and she would not mind a little "demonic possession" if that could embolden her with the impish spirit to shock and shake up the establishment.

Dante's world is fixed and hierarchical, with the one true God eternally at the top in heaven, and the demons, or false pretenders, relegated to hell below. There is only one legitimate faith, and anyone who fails to profess it is damned. Thus all the inhabitants of purgatory, which is the way station between hell and heaven, are like-minded: "In Purgatory they are all Christians, for these souls are heaven-bound, and belief in Christ is a prerequisite" to salvation.[4] Madison, herself unsure about what she believes in, tends to doubt whether heaven ought to be so exclusive. She comments sarcastically that one of the damned is "an Egyptian pharaoh or somebody who went to Hell for praying to the wrong god" (35). Of course, Madison's remarks could be written off as coming from a foolish child; she misquotes the Bible as saying that "it's easier to push caramels through the eye of a needle than get to Heaven" (110). But her naive perspective offers a fresh look at religious doctrine, questioning the rightness of its exclusions. Even her choice of this biblical text—"it is easier for a camel to go through the eye of a needle than for a rich man to enter the kingdom of God"—shows her concern about who is barred from heaven and why.

Against Dante's learned, doctrinaire view of the world as static and stratified, Madison's less informed and still unformed perspective tends toward the dynamic and relativistic. She likes her friend Leonard's theory that "one man's god is another man's devil." In this view, "all the demons of Hell formerly reigned as gods in previous cultures. . . . As each subsequent civilization became a dominant power, among its first acts was to depose and demonize whoever the previous culture had worshiped. . . . As each deity was deposed, it was relegated to Hell" (30–31). If the particular religion that is currently on top is not there because it is right but because it has might, then those who profess other faiths may also have a just claim to heaven. Demons who were once deities could perhaps become gods again; humans unjustly condemned to hell may be able to rise to heaven.

Madison's worldview thus holds out more hope than Dante's. The souls consigned to his Inferno are advised to "*Abandon all hope, ye who enter here*" (184), for they are irrevocably damned. This note is sounded balefully and repeatedly: "Woe to you, corrupted souls! Forget your hope of ever seeing Heaven"; "There is no hope that ever comforts them—no hope for rest and none for lesser pain"; "Among this cruel and depressing swarm, ran people who were terrified, with no hope."[5] But Madison is a self-confessed "hope-aholic" (36). No matter how firmly she is told by the ruling powers that she is forever doomed to hell for her sins, Madison clings to "the H-word [Hope] and the G-word [God]"—proof of her "tenacious addiction to all things upbeat and optimistic" (37). After all, if even such a small infraction as dropping too many cigarette butts on the floor can bring "eternal damnation with no hope for recourse" (211), then why should Madison accept this and other draconian punishments as just? Instead of abandoning all hope, she resolves to "*Abandon all tact*" and rebel against a religious orthodoxy that is so exclusive and punitive (184).

Given Madison's undying hope, her hell starts to seem less like Dante's Inferno of eternally damned souls and more like a nonexclusive version of his Purgatorio, where all souls are able to purge their sins on the way to salvation. Hell—for Madison, as for Dante—is still the place where sinners suffer according to their sins, often enacting the same "negative behavior" they engaged in on Earth, only to "greater and greater extremes, becoming vicious caricatures of themselves, earning fewer and fewer rewards, until they realize their folly" (123). But unlike the damned in Dante's Inferno, for whom any realization they have about themselves is already too late, the souls in Madison's hell have hope of salvation if they learn from their mistakes. Her version of the underworld is more like the Greek Hades or the Jewish Sheol—"Hell as going to detox or rehab instead of Hell as burning punishment" (46). She views hell as "*the place of remorse and remembering*" (152) where people can feel the necessary guilt over their past misdeeds, thus realizing the error of their ways and setting themselves on a path to reform—or, as more bluntly stated in the novel's teenage vernacular, "you stay in Hell until you forgive yourself" for having "fucked up" (181).

By retelling Dante's solemn story from a teen girl's point of view, Palahniuk turns a tragic tale of the damned into a comic narrative of a rebellious spirit who refuses to give up hope. To accomplish this travesty—a parodic imitation of a serious work—Palahniuk crosses Dante with Judy Blume, the author of young-adult fiction whose 1970 novel *Are You There God? It's Me, Margaret* served as inspiration for Madison's voice. Noting that "the Margaret book seemed like such a great example of the form of novel where an innocent person finds themselves thrust into circumstances that are entirely new to them,"[6] Palahniuk is quick to add that, for Madison, "Moving to Hell is way, way worse than Margaret finding herself relocated" from New York to New Jersey.[7] While Margaret has to contend with "*scary*" "*shadows on my wall*" and "*funny creaking sounds*"[8]—"*Please help me God. Don't let New Jersey be too horrible*"[9]—Madison is faced with flames from the fiery pit and the wailing of suffering souls, yet her childhood innocence and her teenage feistiness allow her to remain unfazed. According to Madison, being dead isn't so bad: "crying at my own funeral strikes me as awfully egocentric" (168), and even though "*death has its obvious drawbacks, it is a blessing that I now have an unassailably valid excuse to not take the SATs*" (86). Note the deployment of "awfully" and "*unassailably*" in these last two examples. Palahniuk has said that he favors "adverbs as a useful tool for making horrible scenes funny," for they can "undermine the drama of even the saddest scene."[10] Madison thinks of "life in Hell" as "like a vintage Warner Bros. cartoon where characters are forever getting decapitated by guillotines and dismembered by dynamite explosions, then being completely restored in time for the next assault" (27). Her childhood frame of reference—cartoons, SATs—is absurd in this horribly adult environment; the effect is to make hell seem hilarious and thus bearable.

Madison's situation can be "funny" because "she wasn't really accepting the drama of being dead or the drama of being in hell," explained Palahniuk,[11] adding that further humor comes from her being a rebellious teen too brave or foolhardy to fear the rulers of hell since she considers herself to be their "equal": "When you deny . . . the existing power structure, then comedy occurs."[12] Addressing Satan, Madison tells him that he may be "*synonymous with torment and suffering*" but his "*level of customer service skills really sucks*" (79). Her remark not only reduces the devil to being just another service provider, it also implies that the king of the underworld should be serving *her*. In a fight with Baal, hell's most forbidding demon, Madison conquers him with the "unrelenting volley" of her "infantile slaps and girlish pokes" combined with the "infuriating rain" of her "wet willies and Indian burns" (204). In this mock-epic battle, the demon's power is diminished to that of a grade-school bully, overcome by a teen girl's superior courage. It is no wonder that, when Satan later claims to dictate Madison's actions as if she were a character in a book he had written, she retorts, "*You're not the boss of me,*" adding, "*If anybody wrote me it would be Judy Blume*" (236). Here Palahniuk pays homage to the female novelist who provided the inspiration for his feisty heroine, the counter to Satan's—and Dante's—plot.

As with Blume's "rewrite" of Dante, Palahniuk also has Madison's voice challenge another classic male text—Jonathan Swift's *Gulliver's Travels* (1726)—from the perspective of a more contemporary female author: Alice Walker and *The Color Purple* (1984). While climbing up the body of the demon giantess Pszezpolnica, Madison remembers reading the tale of Gulliver's encounter with the gargantuan ladies of Brobdingnag. The women's great size enables him to see their "naked bodies" up close, provoking in him not desire, but feelings of "horror and disgust": "Their skins appeared so coarse and uneven, so variously coloured, when I saw them near, with a mole here and there as broad as a trencher, and hairs hanging from it thicker than pack-threads." When the ladies lay him on their bosom in order to "have the pleasure of seeing and touching" him, Gulliver is not excited by the proximity, but rather "disgusted" by their "offensive smell."[13] Influenced by her reading, Madison almost has the same disgusted reaction to Pszezpolnica while clambering up that demon's oversized body, "hauling [herself], like Jonathan Swift's worse nightmare, through pungent thickets of curling, dense pubic hair" (75). But Madison suspects that, if Swift and Gulliver think the female sex has a bad smell, it is their own fear and loathing they are projecting. As she comments, "I know the blunt stink of misogyny when I smell it" (73). For Madison has also read the female-affirmative scene in *The Color Purple* where one woman helps another discover the pleasure of her own sexual response. This is what Madison proceeds to do for Pszezpolnica, and as a result the giantess's voracious maw turns into a satisfied and grateful smile. Male disgust is replaced by female bonding, and the demon is defeated not by being destroyed, but by being won over to Madison's side.

This encounter between Madison and Pszezpolnica is not merely incidental, for questions of the body and how to respond to it are at the heart of Palahniuk's novel. Readers can hardly miss the fact that the novel's hell is, as the author puts it, "composed of all the discarded aspects of our physical being: toenail clippings and loose hairs and blood and feces and urine and semen."[14]

One of the generating ideas for hell came from Palahniuk's book tours when he would stay in the authors' suites of hotels and notice not just the autographed books on the shelves, but also the "stray hairs" or "finger clippings" of the writers who had slept there before him: "this juxtaposition of the very physical, the very sort of corrupt body parts of people, next to their thoughts . . . is so fascinating."[15] Here we find Palahniuk wondering at the paradox of eternal souls linked to perishable flesh, for the very same authors whose "minds and hearts are [in books] on the wall"[16]—"people like Jane Fonda and . . . Maya Angelou"—have also left "physical evidence" that they were "mortal beings."[17] As an aging writer himself, Palahniuk has begun to wonder what of him will endure. And should the mortal body be abhorred as the corruptible part of ourselves? Is being encased in flesh a kind of hell—or is there a way of embracing the body as somehow continuous with spirit?

Not merely philosophical, these questions have an even more personal relevance for Palahniuk considering that, during the time in which he wrote this novel, he was tending to his mother's bodily needs—and witnessing her physical suffering—as she was dying of lung cancer. "It was torture, so writing *Damned* was my escape," Palahniuk said. "I'd already found myself in Hell, so why not write about it?"[18] The bodily waste products of the novel's hell take on new meaning if we see them as Palahniuk's attempt to confront his fears about his mother's mortality. As he put it, "Everyone dies, this is something we all have to deal with and it's a shitty shitty thing,"[19] and so "You deal with your shit by writing about shit."[20] Images of waste are not only literally true to the experience of his mother's illness, they also offer something that Palahniuk can exaggerate in fictional form so that the actual circumstances can seem more bearable by comparison: "when you think about the nature of hospitals and sick rooms and that very visceral task I was going through every day for two years—this [writing the novel] was my way of denying the drama I was going through, the shit and blood and urine and vomit. If you expand it to unmanageable proportions [in fiction], you almost reduce it to manageable ones [in reality]."[21]

Exaggeration can also have a comic effect, and by describing the body's deliquescence as "waterfalls of smelly poop" and "*oceans of scalding-hot barf*" (7), Palahniuk can perhaps lighten the severity of the suffering. And choosing a snarky, unfazable young teen as the narrator can help to make a hellish tale more humorous, but now we know the extent to which this narrative is *personal,* concerning as it does the imminent death of the author's mother and the previous passing of his father: "I needed a story that would express my overwhelming grief. No one wants to read a 'requiem novel' where a middle-aged adult mourns dead parents—and that didn't strike me as very fun to write—so I inverted the situation."[22] Palahniuk realized that "a little dead girl who's in hell and really misses her parents but is still kind of plucky and cheerful—that could be funny."[23]

Doomed

In the second book of Palahniuk's Divine Comedy, our thirteen-year-old narrator has left hell and is wandering Earth as a ghost: "Madison is now in Purgatory, dealing with all the dark secrets of her Earthly past," Palahniuk explains.[24] Among these secrets is the reason she was sent to hell in the first place, which was not, as she incorrectly recalls, because she smoked too much marijuana. It was because she killed her grandfather. This death, although not deliberate on Madison's part, was so traumatic that she has repressed it, simultaneously blaming herself and unable to face the severity of her "sin." To purge herself of the "sin," she must remember this terrible event from her past, acknowledge and confess her limited responsibility for it, and thereby earn forgiveness and "salvation." The event occurred when, finding the women's bathroom locked, Madison was forced to use the men's room at a highway rest stop. When a man in the adjoining stall put his erection through a hole in the partition separating them, the uncomprehending girl misread his sexual overture as an attempted assault with a piece of dog poo. Her self-defensive attack on the protruding member caused severe genital injury, from which he eventually bled to death. It was only after inflicting this mortal wound that she discovered the man's identity as her grandfather. Madison has struggled with this awful secret ever since, haunted by half-memories of it and tempted to confess it, but afraid of exposing her guilt and of hurting her family, particularly her grandmother who would not want to know that her husband was a "restroom lurker."[25]

Palahniuk often deals with serious personal issues by exaggerating them in his novels to the point of absurdity, and this restroom incident, while easily dismissed as merely ludicrous—"a panicked public toilet pee-pee mangler" (244)—can be understood as a fictional reworking and a comical condensation of three aspects of his own life. First, there is the event from his past which his family kept secret from him for years: his grandfather murdering his grandmother and then, before killing himself, almost shooting Palahniuk's father, who was at the time only a terrified young boy. The father recalled hiding under a bed, from which he could see only the grandfather's "hobnail logging boots and the muzzle of a gun."[26] Similarly, in the novel's restroom scene, a frightened young Madison hides in the bathroom stall. From under its partition, she can see only her grandfather's "cowboy boots," and through a hole in the stall there protrudes what she takes to be a threatening "finger" (118) or "poo log" (120).

Here, empathizing with what it might have been like for his father to be mortally endangered by the grandfather, Palahniuk somewhat defuses the threat by reimagining it as horrible but hilarious comedy. Madison remains silent about her grandfather's "attack" in an effort to shield her family from the painful truth, and so the incident becomes a dark secret, much like the truth about Palahniuk's grandfather, kept from him and his siblings because "They wanted to protect us."[27]

Second, there is the time when Palahniuk himself was a boy who, after slipping his finger through a washer, got it stuck there, unable to pull it back out. When the finger had grown "swollen and purple,"[28] Palahniuk went to his father who, to teach the boy that his actions had consequences, pretended to chop it off with an ax, missing only at the last moment. Palahniuk kept silent about his father's deed, making it another family secret. In *Doomed,* Palahniuk reverses parent and child to comic effect. It is the grandfather's member which, protruding through the hole in the toilet stall, grows and changes color, and young Madison who attacks what she thinks is a "poo finger" (120), almost dismembering him, especially as he is unable in his swollen state to pull back out through the hole without doing himself further damage. By changing the dismemberer from his father to a young girl, Palahniuk lightens the tone from solemn to silly. Madison's relative innocence—"I may occasionally confuse dog excrement and male genitalia" (181)—tends to reduce her degree of responsibility, and the guilt she feels for attacking her grandfather comes across as comically overblown: "The world would comprehend the penis-lacerating, man-hating murderess she was!" (265).

Third and finally, there is the issue of Palahniuk's homosexuality which, though comically disguised in *Doomed,* is nevertheless connoted by this encounter involving a glory hole in a public restroom. In saying that "what Madison does to her grandfather in a public toilet might make *Doomed* the book that eclipses 'Guts,'"[29] Palahniuk not only draws attention to the shocking scenes in these two works, he also causes us to consider whether there might be a similarity in theme, for both of them deal with sexual shame: guilt over masturbation in "Guts" and embarrassment over homosexuality in *Doomed.* In an interview on the novel, without being asked about sexuality, Palahniuk volunteered that "I'm coming to terms with the enormous embarrassment my parents had about me being homosexual that made our lives uncomfortable and unpleasant and our relationship superficial." He then added, "My way of handling things is to reframe the painful and uncomfortable things and turn them into stories and make them funny. The act of writing is a way of tricking yourself into revealing something that you would never consciously put into the world. Sometimes I'm shocked by the deeply personal things I've put into books without realizing it."[30] The restroom incident in *Doomed* can be read as a seemingly silly but ultimately serious attempt to overcome feelings of shame about homosexuality.

When Madison is compelled to use the men's room because the women's is locked, she feels that her presence there "violated sacred societal taboos" (114). To enter there, she must "abandon every tenet of civilization" and "surrender every moral and ethic [she] held dear" (113). Needless to say, for a young girl to feel this way about going into a men's bathroom is absurd, and yet her degree of guilt seems far less overblown if we consider that the underlying subject here may be homosexual shame. Madison imagines being "severely punished" for her transgression, "stripped" and "flogged" before the "lustful gaze of drooling oafs"—a punishment feared but also "prayed for" (114). This mixture of dread and desire over exhibiting oneself to voyeurs and being pleasurably punished seems in excess of what one is likely to feel about simply using the wrong bathroom. When Madison sees the glory hole in the stall's partition, she thinks of how "Catholics would forget their sins": "they'd talk dirty to God through a hole in the wall." "Pretending to seek divine forgiveness," she then proceeds to "put [her] mouth to the frightening hole" and, in order to "test God's love," confesses to "committing fake murders" (116). Like the "prayed for" punishment, this image condenses desire and shame, sin and the wish for forgiveness. It implies oral sex through the glory hole and at the same time suggests a confession of this "sin" because one has been made to feel ashamed of it. On the one hand, there is the thrill of transgression, the excitement of doing something "dirty" and forbidden, but on the other hand, there is guilt over having "sinned" and the hope of being forgiven and accepted back into God's good graces.

After the restroom incident, Madison feels burdened with a shameful double "secret" that must be "kept": "I'd killed someone. My papadaddy was a restroom lurker" (141). When Madison finds out that the man she killed in the public toilet was in fact her "papadaddy," she has trouble reconciling his "sinful" sexuality with his grandfatherly "goodness," finding herself unable to "resolve the toilet wiener flasher with the Papadaddy who'd taught me how to paint a birdhouse yellow" (141). Here it would seem that Palahniuk has reversed his real-life situation. In actuality, he was the one with the unconventional sexuality causing such "enormous embarrassment"[31] to his parents that they insisted he keep it a secret: "they didn't want it *talked* about. They said: *DON'T TELL ANYONE!*"[32] In the novel, it is the grandparent who is homosexual, as if Palahniuk were asking his parents and grandparents to imagine what it would feel like to be the object of family shame. After all, Palahniuk's grandfather committed murder and Palahniuk's father once threatened dismemberment.

Should the secret of Palahniuk's sexuality be considered so awful when compared to these other dark family secrets?

In the novel's restroom scene, after the grandfather has thrust himself through the glory hole and Madison has mangled his member, she sees him lying on the floor with his "WORLD'S BEST DAD" belt buckle undone and his hand over his crotch, "cupping his shame" (128). She is compelled to ponder how her beloved papadaddy could have a dark, secret side. Later, she imagines seeing "a warped scratched reflection of [herself] in that belt buckle" (133), as if the restroom encounter has provoked her to wonder whether she too has some hidden, "perverted" self. Of course, Madison's secret is ostensibly that she killed her grandfather, but by having her see her own reflection in the man's "splayed open" belt buckle (128), Palahniuk makes an oblique reference to oral sex, as he did earlier in having Madison bring her mouth to the glory hole. This is less a point about Madison than it is about Palahniuk himself, for beneath the ostensible narrative about a girl struggling with guilt over a killing, he is also telling a different story about the attempt to overcome homosexual shame. That is why subsequent scenes will show her fearfully distancing herself from her grandfather's sexuality yet strangely recognizing herself in it. For example, when confronted with the image of her own face formed by his semen on her shirt, she is initially repelled by what she calls "loathsome fluids" and "vile spew": "this is not me. It's wiener juice spurted out. It's the face of a deformed monster" (269). However, Madison will eventually be brought to acknowledge the "monstrous" side of herself.

After being sent to hell and then returning to Earth as a ghost, she finds herself reviled by an identical twin, a perfect "Barbie-Madison" (303) who condemns the real Madison for being a "noxious abomination" (301). In order to fight this accusation, Madison must take on physical form and so, very reluctantly, her spirit enters the body of a recently deceased elderly man. As Madison battles her twin, it seems that a "magic reversal has occurred" (305): instead of her grandfather attacking her, now she, in this mature male body, is the one to "appear as a depraved naked pervert . . . grappling to molest a nude lass," the twin who looks like her former self as a young girl (303). Before, when Madison was that preadolescent girl, it was easy for her to misunderstand and malign adult sexual urges like her grandfather's. Indeed, she used to think of herself as almost a bride of Christ, virginal and pure: "By dating Jesus, I wanted to sidestep all of the blood and spit and sperm that seemed to loom in my immediate future" (261–62). Hence her horror at taking on the form of the elderly man, which she describes in fearful terms as having to "comingle my virginal, intelligent soul" with the "remains of a creepy, predecomposed loser man" (297) and his "vile pendulous *membrum virilis*" (298). But now that Madison finds herself inhabiting the flesh of an adult male, essentially *embodied as her grandfather,* she can understand what it is like to have sexual needs and she can feel sympathy for him and his burden—and for herself and her own budding desires. Madison's battle with her identical twin, the Barbie-Madison, is thus a psychological conflict with her former self, the fearful virgin who condemned adult sexuality as monstrously impure. Against this accusation, the maturing Madison now sides with her grandfather as she realizes that her own growing desires may not be so different from his. If he is "monstrous," then so is she, subject to physical urges that conventional religion and society may view as wrong.

Inhabiting the "sinful" adult body, Madison crawls toward her parents, dragging her "mostly nude, bony, sweat-lubricated self toward them"—a description that strongly suggests an erect phallus (299). At first they mistake her approach for an attack, much as she misunderstood her grandfather's glory-hole advances as an assault. Yet Madison persists in moving toward them, begging them to recognize *her* inside the "atrocity of blood and pus" she is "trapped within"; the reference to engorgement and emission again seems phallic. Her final act is one of lowly entreaty as she makes a groveling appeal for her parents' forgiveness and continued love: "Showing them what a monster I've become, I beg them to accept me" (299–300). While the ostensible reason for needing forgiveness here comes from Madison's having killed her grandfather—a misdeed she confesses in this scene—the phallic subtext implies another motive: Palahniuk's own need to come out into the open about his sexuality and to have his parents accept him for who he is, physically as well as spiritually. In showing her "monstrous" body to her parents, Madison says she is "testing their love" (300), much as earlier she had put her mouth to the glory hole in order to "test God's love" (116). What are these words most crucially about? I would suggest that their underlying meaning concerns the need to express one's sexuality, which might include gay oral sex, without being shunned as a monster by one's family or being excluded from salvation.

Palahniuk employs an innovative literary style in *Doomed*: Madison's tale is told in the form of blog entries written by her ghost. Her blog could function as an updated version of a personal diary in which she reviews her life and unburdens herself of guilt by acknowledging and confessing her darkest secrets. As Madison sees it, if "Purgatory is where you unwrite the book of your life story" (9), then "Writing an honest blog is how you unlive your life" (8). But a blog is not necessarily the place for honest self-examination. Madison struggles with the fact that a blog can just as easily be a refuge or a distraction from the truth about herself.

While engaging in a form of social media, bloggers can often become preoccupied with broad, impersonal matters, such a celebrity gossip, which are unrelated to personal truths. Consider Madison's comment when she finds out that a certain celebrity is upward bound: "give me the strength not to use an emoticon. *Paris Hilton is going to Heaven?* This I can't Ctrl+Alt+Fathom" (29). Madison is tempted to communicate her shock and dismay in a little pictorial representation—perhaps :-O or :-(—that supposedly sums up how she is feeling, or she could use a keyboard shortcut, prefaced by the Ctrl+Alt command, to convey how flabbergasted she is by this bit of news. But these abbreviations for affect are not only inadequate expressions of true emotion, they also beg the question of whether Madison is *feeling* anything at all about this trivial matter. Is she not instead engaging in a social substitute for feeling, a mediated rite known as celebrity gossip?

Although Madison begins each of her blog posts with the salutation "Gentle Tweeter" (8), as if she were continuing the novelistic tradition of addressing each chapter to a Gentle Reader, she eventually comes to believe that there is a difference between the old and the new forms. Novels can devote thousands of words to being deeply personal and introspective. Palahniuk, a novelist who says, "I have never tweeted in my life,"[33] tends to associate blogs with tweets and to be suspicious of both as shorthand forms for conveying socially approved emotions which can be superficial and insincere. Madison gradually senses this distinction. Upon discovering that security cameras once recorded her in the nude, she blogs: "Words Ctrl+Alt+Fail me. Not even emoticons can convey the horror I feel upon hearing this" (43). Madison is being ironic. If words cannot express her feelings, then emoticons most surely will not, for these tiny iconic faces are even more abbreviated and standardized than words. And, if she were not taking such a shortcut or "Ctrl+Alt" approach to communicating her feelings, she might find words that would fail her less often.

Among Madison's strongest feelings is grief over the passing of her grandmother, who dies of lung cancer—as did Palahniuk's mother. Rather than seek help from a grief counselor, Madison adopts a kitten, but it too begins to show signs of disease and impending death. When her father expresses concern, Madison describes him as conveying "Ctrl+Alt+Anxiety" (219). The Internet terminology suggests that she thinks her father is dialing in the emotion, much as later, after the kitten has died and her father orders her to "Flush it. Flush it. *Flush it!*" down the toilet, she describes him as "Ctrl+Alt+Snapping his fingers between each short imperative sentence" (226). Here Madison uses "Ctrl+Alt" as a sign that her father is trying to cut short all feeling; words become a way to distance himself from the emotion of the situation and to hide the truth.

Madison's own blog entries become increasingly ironic as she begins to realize the inadequacy of the very form she is using. While she may feign being "Ctrl+Alt+Nonchalant" about her grandfather's death when she is hoping to hide her role in it from her parents (263), deep down she knows that she must not distance herself from the horrible truth of this event. If she trivializes it by trying to encapsulate it in a brief blog entry as if it were just another piece of scandalous daily news—"Pa Killed in Toilet Torture" (314)—then she will fail to grieve his loss or to admit her own complicity in his demise. Thus she writes that "reducing Papadaddy Ben's death to a blog entry" would be "absurd"—"Mere words. To make you experience the scene fully I'd need to smear his warm dying blood on your hands" (132). The blood metaphor suggests that, as so often in Palahniuk, feeling compassion for someone is experienced as an almost physical connection. The intellect or words are insufficient; true sympathy is bodily. Of course, Madison also has "blood on her hands" in another sense in that she bears some responsibility for her grandfather's death. Rather than repressing the entire event, she must confess her complicity in it so that she can then grieve. Paradoxically, in order to write an "honest blog" (8), she must try to convey what mere words cannot: the physical force of her blood connection to her grandfather, which involves family ties, bodily compassion, and the stain of guilt.

In one of her last posts, Madison is confronted with the challenge of blogging about her reaction to the death of her parents, who have now also passed away. Her address to the reader is telling: "Forgive me, Gentle Tweeter, but what takes place at this juncture is not something one can keyboard. Such are the limitations of emoticons" (323). What she feels cannot be tweeted. The complexity of her emotions exceeds encapsulation in a facial icon. As Madison sees it, blogs can be as distant from deep, personal truths as ghosts are from the living, and so in writing how she feels about her parents' deaths, she tries to connect with the flesh-and-blood truth: "my ghost heart balloons like an aneurysm full of hot tears. It bloats like a deceased kitten in the backseat of a limousine. It's astonishing, but the heart of me engorges like a rapidly inflating, much-turgid man-banana in a fetid toilet. And just like all those things, my heart explodes" (322). The images in this extended simile are all linked around a common action: something that swells to the point of bursting. Burgeoning life—the growth of feeling—and its eventual deflation in death are inextricably part of a continuous process, as are love and grief. Desire in the form of an erection will ultimately lead to loss, as in the bursting of a bloated dead body. Sex and death are interconnected. The fact that Madison has a sympathetic physical response to these images of love and loss is important, for it allows her to *feel* their interconnection in a way that mere intellect or simpler words might not.

Once she has written her confession and purged her earthly sins—including her role in her grandfather's death—Madison will "end up with some kind of salvation," which Palahniuk has said will be the subject of *Delivered,* the third book in his Divine Comedy.[34] One thing is certain: Palahniuk's heaven will not be a place of bloodless abstraction. For him, flesh is not antithetical to spirit. Instead, compassion for the body is proof that one has a soul.

NOTES

Chapter 1—Understanding Chuck Palahniuk

1. Palahniuk, *Invisible Monsters,* 98.
2. Kavanagh, "Of Failed Romance," 189.
3. Palahniuk, "Jane Fonda."
4. Palahniuk, "Power of Persisting."
5. Perry, "All of Creation."
6. Reddit, Comments by Chuck Palahniuk.
7. Adams and Kirtley, "Interview: Chuck Palahniuk."
8. Gambotto-Burke, "Chuck Palahniuk Interview."
9. Reddit, Comments by Chuck Palahniuk.
10. Gambotto-Burke, "Chuck Palahniuk Interview."
11. Palahniuk, "Installing Drivelines," 111.
12. LeVoit, "Interview with Chuck Palahniuk."
13. Hedegaard, "Heart Breaking Life."
14. Palahniuk, "Afterword" to *Fight Club,* 210.
15. Giroux, "Private Satisfactions."
16. Crowdus, "Getting Exercised."
17. Faludi, "It's *Thelma and Louise.*"
18. CNN, "Chuck Palahniuk."
19. Dunne, "About to Choke."
20. Maslin, "Not for a Full Stomach."
21. Maloney, "Demolition Man."
22. Martin, "*Doomed.*"
23. Shone, "Gore Values."
24. O'Kelly, "Sudden Plot Twists."
25. Miller, "*Diary.*"
26. Maslin, "Immature Con Man."
27. Maloney, "Demolition Man."
28. Miller, "*Diary.*"
29. Ibid.
30. Raab, "*Haunted.*"
31. Palahniuk, "Chuck Palahniuk Responds."
32. Hingston, "Interview: Chuck Palahniuk."
33. Tayler, "Foreign Bodies."
34. Valby, "Chuck Palahniuk."
35. Ibid.

36. Staub, "Chuck Palahniuk."
37. Reese, "*Choke*."
38. Daley, "Palahniuk's *Rant*."
39. Shone, "Gore Values."
40. Miller, "*Diary*."
41. Raab, "*Haunted*."
42. Suglia, "*Rant*."
43. Schofelt, "*Damned* If You Do."
44. Martin, "*Doomed*."
45. AbeBooks, "Ranting & Raving."
46. Rosenfeld, "Chuck Palahniuk."
47. Andrews, "Chuck Palahniuk."
48. Parsons, "Gut Check."
49. Houghton, "Chuck Palahniuk Interview."
50. Davies, "Why We All Love."
51. Palahniuk, "Developing a Theme."
52. Palahniuk, *Pygmy*, 56.
53. Farrelly, "Interview with Chuck Palahniuk." Of course, Palahniuk has also written more or less straight journalistic pieces, several of which were published in *Stranger than Fiction: True Stories*.
54. AbeBooks, "Ranting & Raving."
55. Holt, "We Talked about Fight Club."
56. Daley, "Palahniuk's *Rant*."
57. Dee, "Ready-Made Rebellion," 90.
58. Lim, "Crib Notes."
59. Thorne, "Trapped in the Goth Lifestyle."
60. Steinberg, "*Invisible Monsters*," 54.
61. Heffernan, "Name That Tune."
62. Thorne, "Trapped in the Goth Lifestyle."
63. Ellmann, "Love the Ones."
64. Schofelt, "*Damned* If You Do."
65. Churchwell, "Chicken-Chokers' Convention."
66. Palahniuk, "Establishing Your Authority."
67. Houghton, "Chuck Palahniuk Interview."
68. Glassie, "Questions for Chuck Palahniuk," 21.
69. Dowling, "Gonzo Erotica," 47.
70. Jones, "Too Extreme."
71. Victor W. Turner, *The Ritual Process: Structure and Anti-Structure* (Chicago: Aldine Publishing Co., 1969), 96.
72. Ibid., 95.
73. Holt, "We Talked about Fight Club."
74. Borel, "Chuck Palahniuk in Conversation."
75. Palahniuk qtd. in MacDonald, "Chuck Palahniuk."
76. Farley, "Chuck Palahniuk on Oprah's Diaphragm."
77. Suglia, "*Rant*."
78. Suglia, "*Dermaphoria*."
79. Steinberg, "*Fight Club*."
80. New City, "*Invisible Monsters*."

81. Ferguson, "Chuck Palahniuk."
82. Palahniuk, "She Breaks Your Heart."
83. Palahniuk, "Book That Changed My Life," 80.
84. Kavanagh, "Of Failed Romance," 181.
85. Houghton, "Chuck Palahniuk Interview."
86. Widmyer, Kölsch, and Chaplinsky, *Postcards from the Future.*
87. Mookerjee, *Transgressive Fiction,* 2.
88. Hume, *Aggressive Fictions,* 7, 9.
89. Mookerjee, *Transgressive Fiction,* 6.
90. Hume, *Aggressive Fictions,* 83.
91. Catherine Spooner, *Contemporary Gothic* (London: Reaktion Books, 2006), 8.
92. Fred Botting, "Aftergothic: Consumption, Machines, and Black Holes," in *The Cambridge Companion to Gothic Fiction,* ed. Jerrold E. Hogle, 277–300 (New York: Cambridge University Press, 2002), 286.
93. Reddit, Comments by Chuck Palahniuk.
94. Steinberg, "*Fight Club.*"
95. Glassie, "Questions for Chuck Palahniuk," 21.

Chapter 2—The Struggle for Identity

1. Epstein, "Chuck Palahniuk."
2. Farley, "Chuck Palahniuk on Oprah's Diaphragm."
3. Tomlinson, "Is It Fistfighting."
4. Taubin, "So Good It Hurts," 18.
5. Fincher, Director's Commentary.
6. Palahniuk, *Fight Club,* 19, 21. Subsequent citations appear in the text.
7. Palahniuk paraphrased in O'Hagan, "Fright Club."
8. Sheff, "*Playboy* Interview: Chuck Palahniuk."
9. Kleinman, "Chuck Palahniuk."
10. Spear, "Interview with Chuck Palahniuk."
11. Susan Faludi, *Stiffed: The Betrayal of the American Man* (New York: Perennial, 1999), 38.
12. Ibid., 34–35.
13. Stein, "Emasculation Proclamation," 46.
14. Faludi, *Stiffed,* 35.
15. Ibid., 39.
16. Goodlad, "Men in Black," 105.
17. Ibid., 106.
18. Delfino, *Becoming the New Man,* 56.
19. Farley, "Chuck Palahniuk on Oprah's Diaphragm."
20. Brabon, "Spectral Phallus," 64.
21. Giles, "Violence, Spaces," 26.
22. Page One, "Chuck Palahniuk."
23. ShortList, "Chuck Palahniuk."
24. Rugh, "Chuck Palahniuk Is Keeping Portland Strange."
25. Ibid.
26. Palahniuk, "When Giblets Filled the Air," ix.
27. Ibid., x.
28. Palahniuk, "Afterword" to *Fight Club,* 214.

29. Robert Bly, *The Sibling Society* (Reading, MA: Addison-Wesley), 51.
30. Tomlinson, "Is It Fistfighting."
31. Palahniuk, "Afterword" to *Fight Club,* 214.
32. Kavanagh, "Of Failed Romance," 191.
33. Lawless, "Those Burnt Tongue Moments."
34. Reddit, Comments by Chuck Palahniuk.
35. Ibid.
36. Palahniuk, "Tell a Lie, Bury a Gun."
37. Hingston, "Interview: Chuck Palahniuk."
38. Palahniuk, "Talking Shapes: The Rebel."
39. Hingston, "Interview: Chuck Palahniuk."
40. CNN, "Chuck Palahniuk."
41. Kavanagh, "Of Failed Romance," 184.
42. O'Hagan, "Fright Club."
43. Russo, "Lit Interview."
44. Switzer, "From Destruction to Creation."
45. Palahniuk, "Developing a Theme."
46. Palahniuk, *Invisible Monsters,* 55. Subsequent citations appear in the text.
47. Iuliano, "Roaming Captivities," 123.
48. Ash, "Going to the Body," 80.
49. Baelo-Allué, "From Solid to Liquid," 123.
50. Viskovic and Summers-Bremner, "Opposite of a Miracle," 114.
51. Jenkins, "Extreme Sport."
52. Bunn, "Open Book."
53. Reddit, Comments by Chuck Palahniuk.
54. Weston, "Chuck Palahniuk on the Reissue of *Invisible Monsters.*"
55. Palahniuk, *Invisible Monsters Remix,* viii.
56. Switzer, "From Destruction to Creation."
57. Truffin, "'This Is What Passes for Free Will,'" 83.
58. Baelo-Allué, "From Solid to Liquid," 134–35.
59. Johnson, "Bullets and Blades," 71.
60. Switzer, "From Destruction to Creation."
61. Palahniuk, *Invisible Monsters Remix,* 232.
62. Farley, "Chuck Palahniuk on Oprah's Diaphragm."
63. Palahniuk, *Survivor,* 279, 281. Subsequent citations appear in the text.
64. Palahniuk, "Establishing Your Authority."
65. Palahniuk, "Chuck Explains the Ending of *Survivor.*"
66. Spear, "Interview with Chuck Palahniuk."
67. Palahniuk, *Choke,* 169. Subsequent citations appear in the text.
68. Beato, "Heimlich Maneuvers."
69. Epstein, "Chuck Palahniuk."
70. Anderson, "Chuck Palahniuk Interview."
71. Switzer, "From Destruction to Creation."
72. Farley, "Chuck Palahniuk on Oprah's Diaphragm."
73. Blazer, "Phony 'Martyrdom,'" 155.
74. Maslin, "Immature Con Man."
75. Reddit, Comments by Chuck Palahniuk.

76. Dunne, "About to Choke."
77. Palahniuk paraphrased in Straus, "Unexpected Romantic."

Chapter 3—The Horror Trilogy

1. Adams and Kirtley, "Interview: Chuck Palahniuk."
2. Houghton, "Chuck Palahniuk Interview."
3. Russo, "Lit Interview."
4. Nash, "Chuck Palahniuk."
5. Adams and Kirtley, "Interview: Chuck Palahniuk."
6. Kleffel, "*Lullaby.*"
7. Ibid.
8. Ibid.
9. Kavanagh, "Of Failed Romance," 182.
10. Palahniuk, "Freak Speak."
11. Palahniuk, *Lullaby,* 60. Subsequent citations appear in the text.
12. Robertson, "Near-Death Experience."
13. Glassie, "Questions for Chuck Palahniuk," 21.
14. Robertson, "Near-Death Experience."
15. Palahniuk, "Freak Speak."
16. Robertson, "Near-Death Experience." The death sentence was later overturned on a technicality, and Shackleford was sentenced to life in prison.
17. Nash, "Chuck Palahniuk."
18. Sartain, "Interview: Chuck Palahniuk."
19. Robertson, "Near-Death Experience."
20. Nash, "Chuck Palahniuk."
21. Palahniuk, *Diary,* 201. Subsequent citations appear in the text.
22. Walsh, "Chuck Palahniuk Interview."
23. Palahniuk, "Developing a Theme."
24. Palahniuk, "Talking Shapes: The 'Cycle.'"
25. Palahniuk, "Till Death Do Us Part."
26. Walsh, "Chuck Palahniuk Interview."
27. Palahniuk, "Nuts and Bolts."
28. Ibid.
29. Palahniuk, "Till Death Do Us Part."
30. Sartain, "Interview: Chuck Palahniuk."
31. Walker and Wilson, "Chuck Palahniuk Interview."
32. Palahniuk, "Using 'On-the-Body.'"
33. Palahniuk, *Haunted,* 18. Subsequent citations appear in the text.
34. Palahniuk, "'Guts' Effect," 407.
35. Sheff, "*Playboy* Interview: Chuck Palahniuk."
36. Singh, "Chuck Amuck."
37. O'Hagan, "Fright Club."
38. Palahniuk, "Church of Stories."
39. Volmers, "Chuck Palahniuk Tackles God, Death and the Devil."
40. O'Hagan, "Fright Club."
41. Nancy Zapolski and Joe DiMaggio, *Conversations That Matter: Insights & Distinctions—Landmark Essays, Volume 1* (San Francisco: Landmark Education, 2013), 78.

42. Wilma Stassen, "Inside a Landmark Forum Weekend," *Health24*, September 11, 2008, www.health24.com/Mental-Health/Living-with-mental-illness/Inside-a-Landmark-Forum-weekend-20120721 (accessed July 28, 2014).
43. Zapolski and DiMaggio, *Conversations That Matter*, 15, 16, 41.
44. Amelia Hill, "I Thought I'd Be Brainwashed. But How Wrong Could I Be," *Observer*, December 13, 2003, www.theguardian.com/uk/2003/dec/14/ameliahill.theobserver (accessed July 28, 2014).
45. Zapolski and DiMaggio, *Conversations That Matter*, 30, 31.
46. Lawless, "Those Burnt Tongue Moments."
47. Green, "Chuck Palahniuk: 'I'm Not the Werewolf.'"
48. Ibid.

Chapter 4—Teen Terrors

1. Adams and Kirtley, "Interview: Chuck Palahniuk."
2. Palahniuk, *Rant*, 32, 31. Subsequent citations appear in the text.
3. Kleffel, "*Rant*."
4. Ibid.
5. Hedegaard, "Heart Breaking Life."
6. Houghton, "Chuck Palahniuk Interview."
7. Robertson, "Near-Death Experience."
8. Houghton, "Chuck Palahniuk Interview."
9. Kleffel, "*Rant*."
10. Ibid.
11. Metcalfe, "Small Talk."
12. Peitzman, "Interview: Palahniuk Discuses the Nihilism Label."
13. Ibid.
14. AbeBooks, "Ranting & Raving."
15. Ibid.
16. Palahniuk, *Pygmy*, 239, 2, 120, 119. Subsequent citations appear in the text.
17. Suddath, "Novelist Chuck Palahniuk."
18. Ibid.
19. Faber, "Chuck Palahniuk's *Snuff*."
20. Klemer, "Evening with Chuck Palahniuk."
21. Davis, "Live at McNally Robinson."
22. Reddit, Comments by Chuck Palahniuk.
23. Howard, "Chuck Palahniuk at Webster Hall."
24. Reddit, Comments by Chuck Palahniuk.
25. Hingston, "Interview: Chuck Palahniuk."
26. Suddath, "Novelist Chuck Palahniuk."
27. Hingston, "Interview: Chuck Palahniuk."

Chapter 5—Porn Bodies and Romantic Myths

1. Roberts, "*Snuff* Author Chuck Palahniuk."
2. Palahniuk, *Snuff*, 187. Subsequent citations appear in the text.
3. Davies, "Why We All Love."
4. Levy, "*CulturePulp* Q&A."
5. Scieretta, "Interview with Chuck Palahniuk."
6. Kleffel, "2010 Interview."

7. Ibid.
8. Palahniuk, *Tell-All,* 14. Subsequent citations appear in the text.
9. Borel, "Chuck Palahniuk in Conversation."
10. Volmers, "World of Self-Delusion."
11. Neufeld, "Interview with Chuck Palahniuk."
12. Emphasis added in the last three sentences.
13. Hinkle, "Chuck Palahniuk."
14. Powers, "Chuck Palahniuk."
15. Talks, "Chuck Palahniuk."
16. Jabine, "Chuck Palahniuk's *Beautiful You.*"
17. Palahniuk, *Beautiful You,* 7. Subsequent citations appear in the text.
18. E. L. James, *Fifty Shades of Grey* (New York: Vintage Books, 2012), 78.
19. Rugh, "Chuck Palahniuk Is Keeping Portland Strange."
20. Iddamsetty and Koul, "Arcade: Episode 39."
21. Chastain, "Chuck Palahniuk Believes."
22. Smiley, "Novelist Chuck Palahniuk."
23. Iddamsetty and Koul, "Arcade: Episode 39."
24. Rugh, "Chuck Palahniuk Is Keeping Portland Strange."
25. Ibid.
26. Roberts, "*Snuff* Author Chuck Palahniuk."
27. Ayres, "*Fight Club* Author."
28. Iddamsetty and Koul, "Arcade: Episode 39."
29. Jordan Kushins, "Teledildonics: The Weird, Wonderful World of Social Sex Toys," *Gizmodo,* February 7, 2014, gizmodo.com/teledildonics-the-weird-wonderful-world-of-social-sex-1516075707 (accessed November 22, 2014).
30. Iddamsetty and Koul, "Arcade: Episode 39."
31. Green, "Author Chuck Palahniuk."
32. Iddamsetty and Koul, "Arcade: Episode 39."
33. Chastain, "Chuck Palahniuk Believes."
34. See, for example, Palahniuk's statement in McCauley, "*Fight Club* Author": "My parents divorced about the same time the movie *The Parent Trap* came out, about two twins at camp who scheme to get their parents back together. I had that same fantasy."
35. AbeBooks, "Ranting & Raving."

Chapter 6—Palahniuk's Divine Comedy

1. Kleffel, "*Rant.*"
2. Palahniuk, *Damned,* 23. Subsequent citations appear in the text.
3. Hamilton, "Hell, Our Bodies Ourselves."
4. Thomas Goddard Bergin, *Dante's Divine Comedy* (Englewood Cliffs, NJ: Prentice-Hall, 1971), 49.
5. Dante, *The Divine Comedy of Dante Alighieri: Inferno,* trans. Allen Mandelbaum (Berkeley: University of California Press, 1980), III: 84–85; V: 44–45; XXIV: 91–93.
6. Alter, "Chuck Palahniuk Would Like to Take You."
7. Goodreads, "Interview with Chuck Palahniuk."
8. Judy Blume, *Are You There God? It's Me, Margaret* (New York: Dell, 1982), 14.
9. Ibid., 1.
10. Reddit, Comments by Chuck Palahniuk.
11. Sko, "Chuck Palahniuk Transcript."

12. Powers, "*Damned*."

13. Jonathan Swift, *Gulliver's Travels and Other Writings* (Boston: Houghton Mifflin, 1960), 95.

14. Weinstein, "Chuck Palahniuk Goes to Hell."

15. NPR Staff, "*Breakfast Club* Meets Hell."

16. Carpenter, "Chuck Palahniuk Finds Hell."

17. Weinstein, "Chuck Palahniuk Goes to Hell."

18. Daultrey, "Chuck Palahniuk."

19. Sko, "Chuck Palahniuk Transcript."

20. Sammons, "Chuck Palahniuk Interview."

21. Ferguson, "Chuck Palahniuk."

22. Batten, "Chuck Palahniuk Interview."

23. Bennington, "Chuck Palahniuk Interview."

24. Batten, "Chuck Palahniuk Interview."

25. Palahniuk, *Doomed,* 141. Subsequent citations appear in the text.

26. Palahniuk paraphrased in Hedegaard, "Heart Breaking Life."

27. Sheff, "*Playboy* Interview: Chuck Palahniuk."

28. Bunn, "Open Book."

29. Reddit, Comments by Chuck Palahniuk.

30. McCauley, "*Fight Club* Author."

31. Ibid.

32. Gambotto-Burke, "Chuck Palahniuk Interview."

33. Peck, "Chuck Palahniuk." Palahniuk's Twitter account is actually run by Dennis Widmyer, webmaster of the Palahniuk fan site The Cult.

34. Ferguson, "Chuck Palahniuk."

BIBLIOGRAPHY

Books by Chuck Palahniuk

Fight Club. New York: Norton, 1996.
Invisible Monsters. New York: Norton, 1999.
Survivor. New York: Norton, 1999.
Choke. New York: Doubleday, 2001.
Lullaby. New York: Doubleday, 2002.
Fugitives and Refugees: A Walk in Portland, Oregon. New York: Crown, 2003.
Diary. New York: Doubleday, 2003.
Stranger than Fiction: True Stories. New York: Doubleday, 2004.
Haunted. New York: Doubleday, 2005.
Rant: An Oral Biography of Buster Casey. New York: Doubleday, 2007.
Snuff. New York: Doubleday, 2008.
Pygmy. New York: Doubleday, 2009.
Tell-All. New York: Doubleday, 2010.
Damned. New York: Doubleday, 2011.
Invisible Monsters Remix. New York: Norton, 2012.
Doomed. New York: Doubleday, 2013.
Beautiful You. New York: Doubleday, 2014.

Selected Essays by Palahniuk

"Afterword." *Fight Club,* 209–18. New York: Norton, 2005.
"The Book That Changed My Life." *Best Life,* June–July 2008, 80.
"Chuck Explains the Ending of *Survivor.*" *The Cult,* 1999. http://chuckpalahniuk.net/content/chuck-explains-ending-survivor (accessed July 27, 2014).
"Chuck Palahniuk Responds to Laura Miller's Review." *Salon,* August 26, 2003. http://www.salon.com/2003/08/26/chuck_3/ (accessed August 23, 2014).
"A Church of Stories." *Nerve,* April 14, 2005. http://www.nerve.com/personalessays/palahniuk/churchofstories/ (accessed July 28, 2014).
"Developing a Theme." *LitReactor,* September 17, 2011. http://litreactor.com/essays/chuck-palahniuk/developing-a-theme (accessed February 18, 2014).
"Establishing Your Authority." *LitReactor,* September 17, 2011. http://litreactor.com/essays/chuck-palahniuk/establishing-your-authority (accessed February 18, 2014).
"Freak Speak: The Story behind *Lullaby.*" *Randomhouse.com,* December 16, 2002. http://www.randomhouse.com/features/lullaby/story.html (accessed July 27, 2014).
"The 'Guts' Effect: An Afterword (or Warning) of Sorts." *Haunted,* 405–11. New York: Anchor Books, 2006.

"Installing Drivelines." *GQ*, January 2003, 111.

"Jane Fonda Slept Here." *Random House*, October 2011. http://www.byliner.com/chuck-palahniuk/stories/jane-fonda-slept-here (accessed February 1, 2012).

"Nuts and Bolts—The Horizontal versus the Vertical." *LitReactor*, September 16, 2011. http://litreactor.com/essays/chuck-palahniuk/nuts-and-bolts-the-horizontal-versus-the-vertical (accessed February 18, 2014).

"The Power of Persisting: An Introduction." In *Burnt Tongues: An Anthology of Transgressive Stories*, ed. Chuck Palahniuk, Richard Thomas, and Dennis Widmyer. Aurora, IL: Medallion Press, 2014.

"She Breaks Your Heart." *LA Weekly*, September 20, 2002. http://www.laweekly.com/2002-09-26/art-books/she-breaks-your-heart/ (accessed September 10, 2014).

"Talking Shapes: The 'Cycle.'" *LitReactor*, September 15, 2011. http://litreactor.com/essays/chuck-palahniuk/talking-shapes-the-'cycle' (accessed February 18, 2014).

"Talking Shapes: The Rebel, the Follower, and the Witness." *LitReactor*, September 15, 2011. http://litreactor.com/essays/chuck-palahniuk/talking-shapes-the-rebel-the-follower-and-the-witness (accessed February 18, 2014).

"Tell a Lie, Bury a Gun." *LitReactor*, September 15, 2011. http://litreactor.com/essays/chuck-palahniuk/tell-a-lie-bury-a-gun (accessed February 18, 2014).

"Till Death Do Us Part." *Guardian*, May 25, 2006. http://www.theguardian.com/film/2006/may/26/fiction.chuckpalahniuk (accessed July 28, 2014).

"Using 'On-the-Body' Physical Sensation." *LitReactor*, September 17, 2011. http://litreactor.com/essays/chuck-palahniuk/using-"on-the-body"-physical-sensation (accessed February 18, 2014).

"When Giblets Filled the Air: My Introduction to Cacophony." *Tales of the San Francisco Cacophony Society*, ed. Kevin Evans, Carrie Galbraith, and John Law, ix–x. San Francisco: Last Gasp Publishing, 2013.

Selected Interviews with Palahniuk

AbeBooks. "Ranting & Raving with Chuck Palahniuk." *AbeBooks*, 2007. http://www.abebooks.com/docs/authors-corner/chuck-palahniuk.shtml (accessed July 28, 2014).

Adams, John Joseph, and David Barr Kirtley. "Interview: Chuck Palahniuk." *Lightspeed*, no. 21 (February 2012). http://www.lightspeedmagazine.com/nonfiction/feature-interview-chuck-palahniuk/ (accessed July 27, 2014).

Alter, Alexandra. "Chuck Palahniuk Would Like to Take You on a Tour of Hell." *Wall Street Journal Speakeasy*, October 19, 2011. http://blogs.wsj.com/speakeasy/2011/10/19/chuck-palahniuk-would-like-to-take-you-on-a-tour-of-hell/?mod=google_news_blog (accessed August 5, 2014).

Anderson, Jason. "Chuck Palahniuk Interview." *Space Age Bachelor*, March 11, 2001. http://www.space-age-bachelor.com/archives/chuck-palahniu (accessed July 27, 2014).

Andrews, Ed. "Chuck Palahniuk: Inside a Dark Mind." *Huck*, April 22, 2014. http://www.huckmagazine.com/art-and-culture/print/chuck-palahniuk/ (accessed August 25, 2014).

Ayres, Chris. "*Fight Club* Author Chuck Palahniuk Is Talking Dirty." *Times* (London), July 25, 2008. http://livingitfine.blogspot.it/2008/07/fight-club-author-chuck-palahniuk-is.html (accessed November 22, 2014).

Batten, Thomas. "Chuck Palahniuk Interview." *Failbetter*, no. 42 (December 13, 2011). http://www.failbetter.com/42/PalahniukInterview.php (accessed August 5, 2014).

Bennington, Ron. "Chuck Palahniuk Interview on *Ron & Fez—Tell-All*—Part 3 (of 3)." YouTube video, May 28, 2010. https://www.youtube.com/watch?v=UB4VqJ7RoxA&feature=related (accessed August 5, 2014).

Borel, Kathryn. "Chuck Palahniuk in Conversation with Tom Spanbauer." *Believer,* May 2014. http://www.believermag.com/issues/201405/?read=interview_palahniuk_spanbauer (accessed July 28, 2014).

Bunn, Austin. "Open Book." *Advocate,* April 23, 2008. http://www.advocate.com/news/2008/04/23/open-book (accessed July 27, 2014).

Carpenter, Kasey. "Chuck Palahniuk Finds Hell in an Author's Suite." *LitReactor,* October 18, 2011. http://litreactor.com/interviews/chuck-palahniuk-finds-hell-in-an-authors-suite (accessed August 5, 2014).

Chastain, Emma. "Chuck Palahniuk Believes in Hell." *Barnes & Noble Book Blog,* November 4, 2013. http://www.barnesandnoble.com/blog/chuck-palahnuik-believes-in-hell/ (accessed November 22, 2014).

CNN. "Chuck Palahniuk: A Chat about the Novel *Fight Club.*" *CNN.com,* October 27, 1999. http://www.cnn.com/chat/transcripts/palahniuk.html (accessed July 27, 2014).

Daultrey, Stephen. "Chuck Palahniuk: King of the Damned." *Bizarre,* September 2011. http://www.bizarremag.com/film-and-music/interviews/11488/chuck_palahniuk.html (accessed August 5, 2014).

Davies, Adam Lee. "Why We All Love the Idea of Apocalypse." *Time Out,* July 28, 2008. http://www.timeout.com/london/books/chuck-palahniuk-interview (accessed July 28, 2014).

Davis, Brian Joseph. "Live at McNally Robinson: Chuck Palahniuk." Vimeo video, 2009. http://vimeo.com/5296593 (accessed July 28, 2014).

Dowling, Kyle. "Gonzo Erotica: Chuck Palahniuk's Brutal Beauty." *Hustler,* February 2014, 45–49.

Dunne, Kevin. "About to Choke: An Interview with Chuck Palahniuk." *PopMatters,* 2001. http://www.popmatters.com/review/choke/ (accessed July 27, 2014).

Epstein, Dan. "Chuck Palahniuk." *Suicide Girls,* February 14, 2003. https://suicidegirls.com/girls/missy/blog/2678728/chuck-palahniuk/ (accessed July 27, 2014).

Faber, Garrett. "Chuck Palahniuk's *Snuff.*" *Suicide Girls,* May 28, 2008. https://suicidegirls.com/girls/erin_broadley/blog/2679998/chuck-palahniuks-snuff/ (accessed July 28, 2014).

Farley, C. P. "Chuck Palahniuk on Oprah's Diaphragm." *Powell's Books,* July 5, 2001. http://www.powells.com/authors/palahniuk/html (accessed December 15, 2009).

Farrelly, Michael. "An Interview with Chuck Palahniuk." *Bookslut,* June 2004. http://www.bookslut.com/features/2004_06_002656.php (accessed August 26, 2014).

Ferguson, Euan. "Chuck Palahniuk: 'I Wrote the Book While My Mother Was Dying of Cancer.'" *Observer,* September 3, 2011. http://www.theguardian.com/books/2011/sep/04/chuck-palahniuk-fight-club-interview (accessed August 5, 2014).

Gambotto-Burke, Antonella. "The Chuck Palahniuk Interview: The Transcription." In *Mouth.* Broken Ankle Digital, 2013.

Glassie, John. "Questions for Chuck Palahniuk: The Pugilist Novelist." *New York Times Magazine,* September 29, 2002: 21.

Goodreads. "Interview with Chuck Palahniuk." *Goodreads,* May 2010. http://www.goodreads.com/interviews/show/527.Chuck_Palahniuk (accessed August 5, 2014).

Green, Graeme. "Author Chuck Palahniuk on *Fifty Shades of Grey,* Arousal Addiction and Being Visited by the Ghost of His Dad." *Curious Animal,* November 3, 2014. http://www.curiousanimal.com/chuck-palahniuk-interview/ (accessed November 22, 2014).

———. "Chuck Palahniuk: 'I'm Not the Werewolf People Expect.'" *Herald Scotland,* November 24, 2013. http://www.heraldscotland.com/books-poetry/interviews/chuck-palahniu-im-not-the-werewolf-people-expect.22710513 (accessed July 28, 2014).

Hamilton, Brentney. "Hell, Our Bodies Ourselves: Chuck Palahniuk's *Damned.*" *Dallas Observer,* October 18, 2011. http://blogs.dallasobserver.com/mixmaster/2011/10/hell_our_bodies_ourselves_chuc.php (accessed August 5, 2014).

Hedegaard, Erik. "A Heart Breaking Life of Staggering Weirdness." *Rolling Stone,* June 30, 2005.

Hingston, Michael. "Interview: Chuck Palahniuk, *Pygmy.*" *SEE,* May 28, 2009. http://booksinthekitchen.tumblr.com/post/201088424/interview-chuck-palahniuk-pygmy (accessed July 27, 2014).

Hinkle, Ned. "Chuck Palahniuk: *Tell-All.*" YouTube video, September 11, 2012. http://www.youtube.com/watch?v=iuboXWNoF10 (accessed July 28, 2014).

Holt, Devin. "We Talked about Fight Club: Our Interview with Chuck Palahniuk." *SF Weekly,* September 18, 2013. http://www.sfweekly.com/exhibitionist/2013/09/18/we-talked-about-fight-club-our-interview-with-chuck-palahniuk (accessed August 26, 2014).

Houghton, Michael. "Chuck Palahniuk Interview." *Exploding Fist of Death,* 2003. http://www.explodingfistofdeath.com/efod/WR_2003_chuckpalahniuk.php (accessed July 27, 2014).

Howard, Gerry. "Chuck Palahniuk at Webster Hall." YouTube video, May 8, 2009. http://www.youtube.com/watch?v=3nLzBy4a_So (accessed July 28, 2014).

Iddamsetty, Anshuman, and Scaachi Koul. "The Arcade: Episode 39, Featuring Chuck Palahniuk." *Hazlitt,* podcast audio, October 22, 2014. http://penguinrandomhouse.ca/hazlitt/podcast/arcade-episode-39-featuring-chuck-palahniuk (accessed November 22, 2014).

Jabine, Angie. "Chuck Palahniuk's *Beautiful You* Is *Fifty Shades of the Twilight Cave Bear Wears Prada.*" *Oregonian,* October 15, 2014. http://www.oregonlive.com/books/index.ssf/2014/10/chuck_palahniuks_beautiful_you_1.html (accessed November 22, 2014).

Jenkins, Emily. "Extreme Sport: An Interview with Thrill-Seeking Novelist Chuck Palahniuk." *Village Voice,* October 12, 1999. http://www.villagevoice.com/1999-10-12/books/extreme-sport/ (accessed July 27, 2014).

Jones, Philip. "Too Extreme to Read Out Loud?" *Bookseller,* March 30, 2007. http://www.thebookseller.com/profile/too-extreme-be-read-out-loud.html (accessed September 9, 2014).

Kavanagh, Matt. "Of Failed Romance, Writer's Malpractice, and Prose for the Nose: A Conversation with Chuck Palahniuk." In *Sacred and Immoral: On the Writings of Chuck Palahniuk,* ed. Jeffrey A. Sartain, 178–92. Newcastle upon Tyne: Cambridge Scholars Publishing, 2009.

Kleffel, Rick. "*Lullaby,* The Horror Genre." Podcast audio, September 21, 2002. http://trashotron.com/agony/indexes/audio_interview_index.htm (accessed July 27, 2014).

———. "*Rant,* Victor Turner, Science Fiction, Embarrassment." Podcast audio, May 4, 2007. http://trashotron.com/agony/indexes/audio_interview_index.htm (accessed July 28, 2014).

———. "A 2010 Interview with Chuck Palahniuk." Podcast audio, January 20, 2011. http://bookotron.com/agony/news/2011/01-10-11-podcast.htm#podcast011011 (accessed July 28, 2014).

Kleinman, Geoffrey. "Chuck Palahniuk—Author of *Fight Club.*" *DVD Talk,* 2000. http://www.dvdtalk.com/interviews/chuck_palahniuk.html (accessed July 27, 2014).

Klemer, Doron. "An Evening with Chuck Palahniuk." *Doron's Book Blog,* November 22, 2013. http://doronklemer.wordpress.com/2013/11/22/91-an-evening-with-chuck-palahniuk/ (accessed July 28, 2014).

Lawless, Andrew. "Those Burnt Tongue Moments." *Three Monkeys Online,* May 2005. http://www.threemonkeysonline.com/those-burnt-tongue-moments-chuck-palahniuk-in-interview/ (accessed July 27, 2014).

LeVoit, Violet. "An Interview with Chuck Palahniuk." *City Paper,* October 1, 2008. http://www2.citypaper.com/story.asp?id=16792 (accessed August 24, 2014).

Levy, Shawn. "The *CulturePulp* Q&A: Chuck Palahniuk." *CulturePulp,* September 24, 2008. http://culturepulp.typepad.com/culturepulp/2008/09/the-culturepulp-qa-chuck-palahniuk.html (accessed July 28, 2014).

MacDonald, Jay. "Chuck Palahniuk: Going to Extremes." *BookPage,* May 2007. http://bookpage.com/interviews/8406-chuck-palahniuk#.VA-MFmOigqM (accessed September 9, 2014).

McCauley, Mary Carole. "*Fight Club* Author Chuck Palahniuk Returns with *Doomed.*" *Baltimore Sun,* October 5, 2013. http://articles.baltimoresun.com/2013-10-05/entertainment/bs-ae-book-palahniuk-20131005_1_madison-spencer-chuck-palahniuk-fight-club (accessed August 13, 2014).

Metcalfe, Anna. "Small Talk: Chuck Palahniuk." *Financial Times,* July 11, 2009.

Nash, Amanda. "Chuck Palahniuk." *Lollipop,* 2002. http://www.lollipop.com/article.php3?content=issue60/chuckpalahniuk.html (accessed July 27, 2014).

Neufeld, Rob. "Interview with Chuck Palahniuk." *Read on WNC,* April 27, 2010. http://thereadonwnc.ning.com/special/interview-with-chuck-palahniuk?xg_source=activity (accessed July 28, 2014).

NPR Staff. "*The Breakfast Club* Meets Hell in *Damned.*" *NPR Books,* October 16, 2011. http://www.npr.org/2011/10/16/141272918/the-breakfast-club-meets-hell-in-damned (accessed August 5, 2014).

O'Hagan, Sean. "Fright Club." *Observer,* May 7, 2005. http://www.theguardian.com/books/2005/may/08/fiction.chuckpalahniuk (accessed July 27, 2014).

Page One. "Chuck Palahniuk." *Page One Literary Newsletter,* 1999. http://www.pageonelit.com/interviews/ChuckP.html (accessed December 15, 2009).

Parsons, Brad Thomas. "Gut Check: The First Rule of Interviewing Chuck Palahniuk." *Amazon,* 2005. http://www.amazon.com/gp/feature.html?ie=UTF8&docId=564097 (accessed August 25, 2014).

Peck, Claude. "Chuck Palahniuk Goes to Hell." *Vita.mn,* August 9, 2012. http://www.vita.mn/133572443.html?page=all (accessed August 13, 2014).

Peitzman, Louis. "Interview: Palahniuk Discuses the Nihilism Label, Romanticism and Why *Rant* Opened Up New Doors for His Writing." *Daily Californian,* May 10, 2007. http://archive.dailycal.org/article.php?id=24981 (accessed July 28, 2014).

Perry, Kevin E. G. "All of Creation Just Winks Out: Chuck Palahniuk Interviewed." *Quietus,* May 4, 2014. http://thequietus.com/articles/15159-chuck-palahniuk-interview-doomed (accessed August 24, 2014).

Powers, Nicole. "Chuck Palahniuk: *Tell-All.*" *Suicide Girls,* May 26, 2010. https://suicidegirls.com/girls/nicole_powers/blog/2680243/chuck-palahniuk-tell-all/ (accessed July 28, 2014).

———. "*Damned.*" *Suicide Girls,* October 16, 2011. https://suicidegirls.com/girls/nicole_powers/blog/2680394/chuck-palahniuk-damned/ (accessed August 5, 2014).

Reddit. Comments by Chuck Palahniuk. *Reddit,* 2013. http://www.reddit.com/user/ChuckPalahniuk62/comments/ (accessed July 27, 2014).

Roberts, Michael. "*Snuff* Author Chuck Palahniuk Predicts Columbine Porn." *Denver Westworld,* May 21, 2008. http://blogs.westword.com/latestword/2008/05/snuff_author_chuck_palahniuk_p.php (May 28, 2014).

Robertson, Isabella. "Near-Death Experience." *Nerve,* September 13, 2002. http://www.nerve.com/screeningroom/books/interview_palahniuk (February 22, 2014).

Rosenfeld, Jordan E. "Chuck Palahniuk: Shock and Awe." *Writer's Digest,* March 11, 2008. http://www.writersdigest.com/writing-articles/by-writing-genre/literary-fiction-by-writing-genre/the_wd_interview_chuck_palahniuk_shock_and_awe (accessed August 25, 2014).

Rugh, Peter. "Chuck Palahniuk Is Keeping Portland Strange." *Vice,* January 17, 2014. http://www.vice.com/read/chuck-palahniuk-is-keeping-portland-strange (accessed July 27, 2014).

Russo, Charles. "The Lit Interview: Chuck Palahniuk." *Bay Guardian,* 2002. http://www.charlierusso.com/chuck-palahniuk/ (accessed July 27, 2014).

Sammons, Tai. "Chuck Palahniuk Interview." Downpour video, December 21, 2012. http://www.downpour.com/authors/spotlight/chuck-palahniuk-interview/ (accessed August 5, 2014).

Sartain, Jeff. "Interview: Chuck Palahniuk." *Strange Horizons,* October 16, 2006. http://www.strangehorizons.com/2006/20061016/palahniuk-int-a.shtml (accessed July 27, 2014).

Scieretta, Peter. "Interview with Chuck Palahniuk." *SlashFilm,* January 24, 2008. http://www.slashfilm.com/interview-with-chuck-palahniuk/ (accessed July 28, 2014).

Sheff, David. "*Playboy* Interview: Chuck Palahniuk." *Playboy,* May 2009. http://www.playboy.com/playground/view/playboy-interview-chuck-palahniuk (accessed July 27, 2014).

ShortList. "Chuck Palahniuk: Inside the Twisted Brain behind *Fight Club.*" *ShortList,* 2011. http://www.shortlist.com/entertainment/films/chuck-palahniuk (accessed July 27, 2014).

Sko, Allan. "Chuck Palahniuk Transcript." *BMA Magazine,* September 27, 2011. http://bmamag.com/articles/features/20110926-chuck-palahniuk-transcript/ (accessed August 5, 2014).

Singh, Gary. "Chuck Amuck." *Metroactive,* May 18, 2005. http://www.metroactive.com/papers/metro/05.18.05/palahniuk-0520.html (accessed July 28, 2014).

Smiley, Tavis. "Novelist Chuck Palahniuk." *Tavis Smiley,* PBS video, May 28, 2010. http://www.pbs.org/wnet/tavissmiley/interviews/novelist-chuck-palahniuk/ (accessed July 28, 2014).

Spear, Ryan. "An Interview with Chuck Palahniuk." *Portland Review Literary Journal,* 2000. http://poeticalo.tripod.com/PoeticaLZinE/id2.html (accessed July 27, 2014).

Staub, Dick. "Chuck Palahniuk." *Christianity Today,* October 1, 2002. http://www.christianitytoday.com/ct/2002/octoberweb-only/10-7-21.0.html?paging=off (accessed August 23, 2014).

Stein, Joel. "The Emasculation Proclamation." *Time,* October 25, 1999: 46.

Straus, Tamara. "The Unexpected Romantic: An Interview with Chuck Palahniuk." *AlterNet,* June 18, 2001. http://www.alternet.org/story/11049/the_unexpectedromantic%3A_an_interview_with_chuck_palahniuk (accessed July 27, 2014).

Suddath, Claire. "Novelist Chuck Palahniuk." *Time,* May 12, 2009. http://content.time.com/time/arts/article/0,8599,1897504,00.html (accessed July 28, 2014).

Switzer, Chris. "From Destruction to Creation: Chuck Palahniuk Discusses *Choke* and His Writing." *turtleneck.net,* August 12, 2001. http://dusan.satori.sk/i/txt/palahniuk01.php (accessed July 27, 2014).

Talks. "Chuck Palahniuk: 'You Can't Just Be a Spectator.'" *The Talks,* November 5, 2014. http://the-talks.com/interviews/chuck-palahniuk/ (accessed November 22, 2014).

Tomlinson, Sarah. "Is It Fistfighting, or Just Multi-Tasking?" *Salon,* October 13, 1999. http://www.salon.com/1999/10/13/palahniuk/ (accessed July 27, 2014).

Valby, Karen. "Chuck Palahniuk Does Not Attend Fight Club." *Entertainment Weekly,* September 26, 2003. http://www.ew.com/ew/article/0,,488215,00.html (accessed August 23, 2014).

Volmers, Eric. "Chuck Palahniuk Tackles God, Death and the Devil in *Doomed.*" *Calgary Herald,* October 17, 2013.

———. "A World of Self-Delusion: Palahniuk Skewers Hollywood in Funny, Dark *Tell-All.*" *Ottawa Citizen,* June 27, 2010. http://www2.canada.com/ottawacitizen/news/archives/story.html?id=35e0ff4f-df49-4532-b5c6-4d9fb47df213 (accessed July 28, 2014).

Walker, James, and Jared Wilson. "Chuck Palahniuk Interview." *LeftLion,* October 2, 2008. http://www.leftlion.co.uk/articles.cfm/title/chuck-palahniuk-interview/id/2296#.Uuw6YrSCAqM (accessed July 28, 2014).

Walsh, Jeff. "Chuck Palahniuk Interview." *JeffWalsh.com,* February 22, 2003. http://jeffwalsh.com/2003/02/22/chuck-palahniuk-interview/ (accessed July 28, 2014).

Weinstein, Adam. "Chuck Palahniuk Goes to Hell." *Mother Jones,* November–December 2011. http://www.motherjones.com/media/2011/10/chuck-palahniuk-interview-damned (accessed August 5, 2014).

Weston, Hillary. "Chuck Palahniuk on the Reissue of *Invisible Monsters.*" *BlackBook,* June 2012. http://www.bbook.com/chuck-palahniuk-on-the-reissue-of-invisible-monsters/ (accessed July 27, 2014).

Widmyer, Dennis, Kevin Kölsch, and Josh Chaplinsky, dirs. *Postcards from the Future: The Chuck Palahniuk Documentary.* Kinky Mule Films, DVD, 2003.

Selected Works about Palahniuk

Ash, Scott. "Going to the Body: The Tension of Freedom/Restraint in Palahniuk's Novels." In *Sacred and Immoral: On the Writings of Chuck Palahniuk,* ed. Jeffrey A. Sartain, 73–88. Newcastle upon Tyne: Cambridge Scholars Publishing, 2009.

Baelo-Allué, Sonia. "From Solid to Liquid: *Invisible Monsters* and the Blank Fiction Road Story." In *Chuck Palahniuk: Fight Club, Invisible Monsters, Choke,* ed. Francisco Collado-Rodríguez, 117–35. New York: Bloomsbury, 2013.

Beato, G. "Heimlich Maneuvers." *Washington Post,* May 27, 2001. http://www.soundbitten.com/choke.html (accessed July 27, 2014).

Blazer, Alex E. "The Phony 'Martyrdom of Saint Me': *Choke, The Catcher in the Rye,* and the Problem of Narcissistic Nihilism." In *Reading Chuck Palahniuk: American Monsters and Literary Mayhem,* ed. Cynthia Kuhn and Lance Rubin, 143–56. New York: Routledge, 2009.

Brabon, Benjamin A. "The Spectral Phallus: Re-Membering the Postfeminist Man." In *Postfeminist Gothic: Critical Interventions in Contemporary Culture,* ed. Benjamin A. Brabon and Stéphanie Genz, 56–67. New York: Palgrave Macmillan, 2007.

Churchwell, Sarah. "Chicken-Chokers' Convention." *Guardian,* August 15, 2008. http://www.theguardian.com/books/2008/aug/16/chuckpalahniuk.fiction (accessed September 9, 2014).

Crowdus, Gary. "Getting Exercised over *Fight Club.*" *Cineaste* 25, no. 4 (Fall 2000): 46–48.

Daley, David. "Palahniuk's *Rant* Fails to Draw Many Raves." *USA Today,* May 7, 2007. http://www.usatoday.com/story/life/books/2013/06/28/palahniuks-rant-fails-to-draw-many-raves/2468145/ (accessed September 8, 2014).

Dee, Jonathan. "Ready-Made Rebellion: The Empty Tropes of Transgressive Fiction." *Harper's,* April 2005, 87–91.

Delfino, Andrew Steven. *Becoming the New Man in Post-Postmodernist Fiction: Portrayals of Masculinities in David Foster Wallace's Infinite Jest and Chuck Palahniuk's Fight Club.* Saarbrücken, Germany: VDM Verlag Dr. Müller, 2008.

Ellmann, Lucy. "Love the Ones You're With." *New York Times Book Review,* June 8, 2008.

Faludi, Susan. "It's *Thelma and Louise* for Guys." *Newsweek,* October 25, 1999: 89.

Fincher, David. Director's Commentary. *Fight Club,* 10th Anniversary Edition Blu-ray DVD. Twentieth Century Fox Home Entertainment, 2009.

Giles, James R. "Violence, Spaces, and a Fragmenting Consciousness in *Fight Club.*" In *Chuck Palahniuk: Fight Club, Invisible Monsters, Choke,* ed. Francisco Collado-Rodríguez, 23–43. New York: Bloomsbury, 2013.

Giroux, Henry A. "Private Satisfactions and Public Disorders: *Fight Club,* Patriarchy, and the Politics of Masculine Violence." *Journal of Advanced Composition* 21, no. 1 (Winter 2001): 1–31.

Goodlad, Lauren M. E. "Men in Black: Androgyny and Ethics in *The Crow* and *Fight Club.*" In *Goth: Undead Subculture,* ed. Lauren M. E. Goodlad and Michael Bibby, 89–118. Durham: Duke University Press, 2007.

Heffernan, Virginia. "Name That Tune." *New York Times Book Review,* October 20, 2002.

Hume, Kathryn. *Aggressive Fictions: Reading the Contemporary American Novel.* Ithaca: Cornell University Press, 2012.

Iuliano, Fiorenzo. "Roaming Captivities: Assembling Bodies and Territories in Chuck Palahniuk's *Invisible Monsters.*" In *Queerdom: Gender Displacements in a Transnational Context,* ed. Mario Corona and Donatella Izzo, 107–26. Bergamo, Italy: Bergamo University Press, 2009.

Johnson, Andy. "Bullets and Blades: Narcissism and Violence in *Invisible Monsters.*" In *Sacred and Immoral: On the Writings of Chuck Palahniuk,* ed. Jeffrey A. Sartain, 61–72. Newcastle upon Tyne: Cambridge Scholars Publishing, 2009.

Lim, Dennis. "Crib Notes." *Village Voice,* November 19, 2002. http://www.villagevoice.com/2002-11-19/books/crib-notes/ (accessed September 8, 2014).

Maloney, Field. "Demolition Man." *New York Times Book Review,* June 3, 2007.

Martin, Tim. "*Doomed.*" *Telegraph,* November 11, 2013. http://www.telegraph.co.uk/culture/books/bookreviews/10433985/Doomed-by-Chuck-Palahniuk-review.html (accessed August 22, 2014).

Maslin, Janet. "An Immature Con Man with a Mom Problem." *New York Times,* May 24, 2001.

———. "Not for a Full Stomach (or an Empty One Either)." *New York Times,* May 5, 2005.

Miller, Laura. "*Diary.*" *Salon,* August 20, 2003. http://www.salon.com/2003/08/20/palahniuk_3/ (accessed August 23, 2014).

Mookerjee, Robin. *Transgressive Fiction: The New Satiric Tradition.* New York: Palgrave Macmillan, 2013.

New City. "*Invisible Monsters.*" *New City,* 1999. http://books.wwnorton.com/books/detail.aspx?ID=6580 (accessed September 10, 2014).

O'Kelly, Kevin. "Sudden Plot Twists Leave *Rant* Empty." *Boston Globe,* May 16, 2007. http://www.boston.com/ae/books/articles/2007/05/16/sudden_plot_twists_leave_rant_empty/ (accessed August 23, 2014).

Raab, Scott. "*Haunted.*" *Esquire,* June 2005, 42.

Reese, Jennifer. "*Choke.*" *New York Times Book Review,* May 27, 2001.

Schofelt, Christine. "*Damned* If You Do." *World Socialist Web Site,* January 4, 2012. http://www.wsws.org/en/articles/2012/01/damn-j04.html (accessed August 25, 2014).

Shone, Tom. "Gore Values." *New York Times Book Review,* May 22, 2005.

Steinberg, Sybil S. "*Fight Club.*" *Publisher's Weekly,* June 3, 1996: 60.

———. "*Invisible Monsters.*" *Publisher's Weekly,* July 5, 1999: 54.

Suglia, Joseph. "*Dermaphoria.*" *DrJosephSuglia.* https://drjosephsuglia.wordpress.com/tag/palahniuk/ (accessed September 10, 2014).

———. "*Rant.*" *DrJosephSuglia.* http://drjosephsuglia.wordpress.com/2013/07/11/rant-by-chuck-palahniuk/ (accessed August 25, 2014).

Taubin, Amy. "So Good It Hurts." *Sight and Sound* 9 (November 1999): 18.

Tayler, Christopher. "Foreign Bodies." *Guardian,* June 12, 2009. http://www.theguardian.com/books/2009/jun/13/pygmy-chuck-palahniuk-review (accessed August 23, 2014).

Thorne, Matt. "Trapped in the Goth Lifestyle?" *Independent,* May 13, 2007. http://www.independent.co.uk/arts-entertainment/books/reviews/rant-by-chuck-palahniuk-448670.html (accessed February 1, 2008).

Truffin, Sherry. "'This Is What Passes for Free Will': Chuck Palahniuk's Postmodern Gothic." In *Reading Chuck Palahniuk: American Monsters and Literary Mayhem,* ed. Cynthia Kuhn and Lance Rubin, 73–87. New York: Routledge, 2009.

Viskovic, Richard, and Eluned Summers-Bremner. "The Opposite of a Miracle: Trauma in *Invisible Monsters.*" In *Chuck Palahniuk: Fight Club, Invisible Monsters, Choke,* ed. Francisco Collado-Rodríguez, 97–115. New York: Bloomsbury, 2013.

INDEX

1984 (Orwell), 12

Abbey, Edward, 12
Adbusters, 51
Adventures of Huckleberry Finn, The (Twain), 12, 69, 101
Adventures of Tom Sawyer, The (Twain), 69, 101
All That Jazz (Fosse), 83
American Psycho (Ellis), 12
America's Next Top Model, 35
Andy Griffith Show, The, 99
Angelou, Maya, 107
Are You There God? It's Me, Margaret (Blume), 105–6
Ash, Scott, 29
Auel, Jean M., 95

Baelo-Allué, Sonia, 30, 34
Barker, Clive, 12
Barrel Fever (Sedaris), 11
Bauhaus, 14
Beato, G., 42
Beautiful You (Palahniuk), 4, 9, 81, 93–100, 101
"Bela Lugosi's Dead" (Bauhaus), 14
Bernstein, Carl, 2
Blair Witch Project, The (Sánchez and Myrick), 8
Blazer, Alex E. 48
Blume, Judy, 105–6
Bly, Robert, 21
Books of Blood, The (Barker), 12
Boreman, Linda, 82
Bostonians, The (James), 15
Botting, Fred, 13
Brabon, Benjamin A., 19
Bradbury, Ray, 12
Breakfast at Tiffany's (Capote), 12, 15
Burbank, 1
Burning Man, 8
burnt tongue, 7

Cacophony Society, 20
Campfires of the Dead (Christopher), 11
Capote, Truman, 15
Carrie (King), 12, 82
Cartland, Barbara, 96
Carver, Raymond, 11
chick lit, 4, 94–95
Choke (Palahniuk), 4, 7, 8, 9, 10, 14, 15, 42–49, 81, 92
Chong, Annabel, 81
Christopher, Peter, 11
Cinderella, 24, 28, 35, 95
Citizen Kane (Welles), 8
Clan of the Cave Bear, The (Auel), 95
Color Purple, The (Walker), 106
Columbine massacre, 21, 77
Crazy Salad (Ephron), 11
"Creep" (Radiohead), 14
crowd-seeding, 8
Crowdus, Gary, 3

Damned (Palahniuk), 4, 9, 10, 81, 101–8
Dante, 101–6
Day of the Locust, The (West), 12
Deep Throat (Damiano), 82
Delfino, Andrew Steven, 19
Delivered (Palahniuk), 115
Depeche Mode, 14
Devil Wears Prada, The (Weisberger), 94, 95

Diary (Palahniuk), 4, 7, 9, 13, 14, 56–61, 81
Diaz, Junot, 11
Dick, Philip K., 12
Didion, Joan, 11
Divine Comedy (Dante), 101–6
Doomed (Palahniuk), 4, 9, 13, 81, 101, 108–15
Dora (Yuknavitch), 12
Drown (Diaz), 11
Dunn, Katherine, 12

Eleanor of Aquitaine, 89
Ellis, Bret Easton, 11, 12
Ephron, Nora, 11
Exorcist, The (Friedkin), 103

factoids, 8
Faludi, Susan, 3, 17
Fifty Shades of Grey (James), 94, 95
Fight Club (film), 3, 15–16, 26–27
Fight Club (Palahniuk), 3–5, 7, 8, 9, 10, 13, 14, 15–27, 36, 42, 47, 50, 81
Fight Club 2 (Palahniuk), 4
Fincher, David, 15, 16
Fitzgerald, F. Scott, 15
Fonda, Jane, 13, 107
Foucault, Michel, 29
Frawley, William, 89
Freightliner Trucks, 2, 6

Garbo, Greta, 90
Geek Love (Dunn), 12
Giles, James R., 19
Giroux, Henry A., 3
Gizmodo, 97
going on the body, 6, 62
Gone with the Wind (Mitchell), 12
gonzo-erotica, 96, 98–99
Goodbye to Berlin (Isherwood), 12
Goodlad, Lauren M. E., 18
Graduate, The (Nichols), 13–14
Great Gatsby, The (Fitzgerald), 12, 15
Gulliver's Travels (Swift), 106
"Guts" (Palahniuk), 61–63, 101, 109

Hammett, Dashiell, 16
Happy Days, 99
Harold and Maude (Ashby), 14
Haunted (Palahniuk), 4, 9, 10–11, 13, 14, 61–67
Haunting of Hill House, The (Jackson), 12
Hemingway, Ernest, 11
Hempel, Amy, 11
Hepburn, Katharine, 87
Hershey, Barbara, 83
Hilton, Paris, 113
Homes, A. M., 11
horror, 4, 13, 50, 56, 60–61
horses, 7
Houellebecq, Michel, 12
Howard, Ron, 99
Hume, Kathryn, 12–13

Ice at the Bottom of the World, The (Richard), 11
Idol, Billy, 14
Ill Nature (Williams), 11
Inferno (Dante), 101–6
Informers, The (Ellis), 11
Invisible Monsters (Palahniuk), 1, 4, 7, 8, 9, 10, 13, 15, 16, 27–36, 42, 81
Invisible Monsters Remix (Palahniuk), 10, 34, 35–36, 81
Iuliano, Fiorenzo, 28

Jackson, Shirley, 12, 62
James, Henry, 15
"Jane Austen's Fight Club" (video), 3
Janowitz, Tama, 11
Jesus' Son (Johnson), 11
Johnson, Andy, 35
Johnson, Denis, 11
Jones, Thom, 11

Kelly, Grace, 87, 90
King, Stephen, 12, 82
Klute (Pakula), 13

Landmark Forum, 3, 64–66
Levin, Ira, 12, 50
Lish, Gordon, 11
"Little 15" (Depeche Mode), 14
"Lottery, The" (Jackson), 12, 62
Lovelace, Linda, 82
Lullaby (Palahniuk), 4, 7, 9, 10, 13, 14, 51–56, 81

Maloney, Field, 4
Martian Chronicles, The (Bradbury), 12
Martin, Tim, 4
Maslin, Janet, 4, 48
Messalina, 83
Meyer, Stephenie, 95
Millay, Edna St. Vincent, 89
minimalism, 7, 11
Miss America, 35
Monkey Wrench Gang, The (Abbey), 12, 50
Monroe, Marilyn, 86, 93
Mookerjee, Robin, 12–13
Moyers, Bill, 21

New Yorker, 62
Night Shift (King), 12
Nine Inch Nails, 14
nonfiction forms, 8

One Flew Over the Cuckoo's Nest (Kesey), 12
Ordeal (Lovelace and McGrady), 82
Oregon, University of, 2
Orwell, George, 12

Palahniuk, Carol (mother), 2, 73, 87, 96, 97, 98, 107, 109–10, 112, 113, 123n34
Palahniuk, Chuck: and 9/11 attacks, 27, 50, 51, 68; on aging, 27–28; book tours, 61–63, 90, 107; and bullying, 77; childhood, 1–2; critics of, 4–6, 8–9, 42; and death penalty, 52–53, 121n16; films, influence of, 13–14, 73; homosexuality, 33, 109–12; journalism degree, 2, 8, 102; learning to read and write, 1–2, 76; literary tradition, 11–12, 15; protagonists, 12; readers of, 5–6; as satirist, 9, 12–13; social experiments, 10–11, 21; songs, influence of, 14; style, 6–8; at soup kitchen, 75; at support groups, 16; therapeutic fiction, 9, 63–67; Ukrainian relatives, 76; work as a mechanic, 2–3, 19; and writers' group, 64, 67, 85
Palahniuk, Fred (father), 1, 2, 48, 52, 72–73, 95–96, 98, 107, 108–10, 112, 123n34
Palahniuk, Nick (paternal grandfather), 2, 72–73, 108–10
Palahniuk, Paula (paternal grandmother), 2, 72, 108
Paradiso (Dante), 101
Parent Trap, The (Swift), 123n34.
Pasco, 1
Picture of Dorian Gray, The (Wilde), 92
Platform (Houellebecq), 12
Poe, Edgar Allan, 12
Portland, 2, 20
Pretty Woman (Marshall), 36
Pugilist at Rest, The (Jones), 11
Purgatorio (Dante), 101, 104
Pygmy (Palahniuk), 4, 7, 9, 10, 14, 68, 75–80, 81, 101

Queen, Ellery, 11

Radiohead, 14
Rand, Ayn, 5
Rant (Palahniuk), 4, 8, 9, 10, 12, 13, 68–74, 75, 81, 82, 101
Richard, Mark, 11
Roberts, Julia, 84
Rosemary's Baby (Levin), 12, 50

Sade, Marquis de, 96
Safety of Objects, The (Homes), 11
San Francisco, 20
Santa Rampage, 20
Schwarzenegger, Arnold, 18
science fiction, 4, 12, 67
Seattle World's Fair, 1
Sedaris, David, 11
Sex: The Annabel Chong Story (Lewis), 81
Shackleford, Dale, 52–53, 121n16
Sibling Society, The (Bly), 21
Slaughterhouse-Five (Vonnegut), 12
Slaves of New York (Janowitz), 11
Slouching Towards Bethlehem (Didion), 11
Snuff (Palahniuk), 4, 8, 9, 10, 81–87, 93
Spanbauer, Tom, 6–7, 11, 62
Spooner, Catherine, 13
Steinbeck, John, 11
Stepford Wives, The (Levin), 12, 50
Stiffed (Faludi), 17, 18
Stranger than Fiction: True Stories (Palahniuk), 118n53

Summers-Bremer, Eluned, 30
Sundance Film Festival, 92
Survivor (Palahniuk), 4, 8, 9, 10, 13, 15, 16, 36–42, 50, 81
Swift, Jonathan, 106

Tayler, Christopher, 5
teledildonics, 97–98
Tell-All (Palahniuk), 4, 9, 13, 81, 87–93, 95
They Shoot Horses, Don't They? (Pollack), 13
Thoreau, Henry David, 69
Trainspotting (Welsh), 12, 50
transgressive fiction, 12, 50, 67
Truffin, Sherry R., 34
Turner, Victor, 10
Twain, Mark, 12
Twilight (Meyer), 95

Uhls, Jim, 16

Valley of the Dolls (Susann), 12
Viskovic, Richard, 30
Vogue, 34
Vonnegut, Kurt, Jr., 12

Walker, Alice, 106
Watergate, 2
Welsh, Irvine, 12
West, Nathanael, 12
Widmyer, Dennis, 124n33
Williams, Joy, 11
Woodward, Bob, 2
World's Biggest Gang Bang, The (Bone), 81

Yuknavitch, Lidia, 12

zombie, 74